Single Parenting

Single Parenting

Wisdom and Hope for the Journey

AUGUSTA ADESOLA OGUNYEMI

Copyright © 2023

All rights reserved.

No part of this book may be reproduced in any form or by any electronic or mechanical means, including information storage and retrieval systems, without written permission from the author, except for the use of brief quotations in a book review.

ISBN: 9798860454293

The Bible versions used include:

Amplified Bible, Classic Edition (AMPC) Copyright © 1954, 1958, 1962, 1964, 1965, 1987 by The Lockman Foundation; **King James Version (KJV)** Public Domain; **New International Version (NIV)** Holy Bible, New International Version®, NIV® Copyright ©1973, 1978, 1984, 2011 by Biblica, Inc.® Used by permission. All rights reserved worldwide.; **New King James Version (NKJV)** Scripture taken from the New King James Version®. Copyright © 1982 by Thomas Nelson. Used by permission. All rights reserved.; and **New Living Translation (NLT)** *Holy Bible*, New Living Translation, copyright © 1996, 2004, 2015 by Tyndale House Foundation. Used by permission of Tyndale House Publishers, Inc., Carol Stream, Illinois 60188. All rights reserved;

CONTENTS

Foreword ... vii
Rev. Dr Johnson Abimbola & Rev. Dr Dee Abimbola

Preamble ... xi

PART ONE
GOD'S DIVINE PLAN FOR THE HOME

1. God's Design for Marriage and Family ... 3
2. Why Single Parenting Was Not Intended by God ... 11
3. Single Parenthood in Historical Context ... 19
4. Diverse Pathways Into Single Parenthood ... 31
5. Single Parenting and the Society ... 39
6. The Crucial Interplay of Father and Mother in a Well-Balanced Home ... 45
   The Body Analogy

PART TWO
PRACTICAL INSIGHTS FOR SINGLE PARENTS

7. Navigating Your New Reality and Family Dynamics in Single Parenthood ... 53
8. Navigating the Impact of Single Parenting on Children ... 65
9. You Need Help ... 71
10. Approaches to Discipline in Single Parenting ... 87
11. Embracing Change ... 99
12. Relationship with the Children in this Digital Age ... 103

13. Your Future Relationship with Your Exes — 109
14. The Complexity of Second Marriages — 117

PART THREE
RESTORATION AND HEALING

15. On Your Way To Recovery — 123
16. Overcome Your Fear — 133
17. Wisdom: The Essential Requirement for Every Single Parent — 141
18. Reconciliation — 145

About the Book — 149
About the Author — 151

FOREWORD
REV. DR JOHNSON ABIMBOLA & REV. DR DEE ABIMBOLA

Our first meeting with Elder Augusta Adesola Ogunyemi in 2003 was God-ordained and germane to the subject matter of *Single Parenting: Wisdom and Hope for the Journey*. The unplanned meeting point was the entrance of the students' hall of residence, Liverpool Hope University. We approached a woman standing near the door to help us in our search for Kemi-Bukky, a sister from Nigeria who we understood lived there. Imagine the joy that filled our hearts when Elder Ogunyemi told us that the lady we were looking for is her daughter!

Having known Elder Augusta for upwards of twenty years, we are confidently saying that she is eminently qualified to discuss thorny issues surrounding single parenting. Not only has her life demonstrated Christian virtues of Godliness, integrity and resilience, she has also been an epitome of faith in the face of tribulation. As pastors of Elder Augusta, she earned our deep respect as a woman who sacrificed her comfort, pleasure and indeed her entire life for ALL her children. Elder Augusta's virtue of extreme Christian selflessness, which is the hallmark of single parenting, is demonstrated in every facet of her relationships. Her eagerness to support every family to be the best version of themselves drives her service in the Church and Community, and mostly in her desire to see generations coming behind avoiding the pitfalls that may negatively impact their lives.

In her usual no-nonsense, honest Christian approach, Elder Augusta makes it clear that God's way is the best way – that is, Father and Mother joining hands to bring up Children in a loving family environment. However, making it clear that life circumstances may put people in a 'New Reality' of Single Parenthood, she sympathetically offers Godly and practical insights into how single parents could navigate the often-precarious pathways of life. While encouraging single parents not to discard support from relatives, Church and community, she points them to the ultimate source of help, which is God

Our hearts' desire is that no one misses out on the deep treasure that has come out of the life story of Elder Augusta as reflected in *Single Parenting: Wisdom and*

Hope for the Journey, who has poured herself out as water, resting on God's grace *"who comforts us in all our tribulations, that we may be able to comfort those who are in any trouble by the comfort with which we ourselves are comforted of God"* (2 Corinthians 1:4).

We strongly recommend this book, therefore, in the name of our Lord Jesus Christ, as an essential guide, first and foremost, to the direct beneficiaries — single mothers (and fathers). Secondly, this book is a must-read for adult children brought up in single-parent families. It will help to resolve some of the complex issues and concerns they had growing up. It could also help to bring closure to some issues. Thirdly, we recommend this book to all parents and parents-to-be who may find themselves in a position to utilise the vast knowledge and experience demonstrated by the author to support single parents around them. All in all, this book is an essential read for government policymakers in the Social Sector, Pastors, Christians and all who are awaiting the coming of the Lord.

Rev. Dr Johnson Abimbola & Rev. Dr Dee Abimbola
Alive Believers Church
259-261 Boaler Street
Liverpool L6 9DH

PREAMBLE

Becoming a parent does not automatically make one knowledgeable to bring up a child. It is a skill that has to be learnt at the 'University of Life'. Parenting is one of the core courses, and it is not optional. Sadly, quite a number of people fail this course woefully. Most repeat the course after bitter experiences. People fail the course because of levity or because they think the course is simple. Most have not got the necessary requirements to enrol on the course. Having money, influence or academic excellence does not qualify one to begin and finish well.

Every child is born into this world that is ripped through by moral and spiritual decadence the same way, irrespective of parental status, whether a prince or a pauper's child. However, differences begin to set in as a result of the type of parenting they get. Largely, children follow their parents' examples and may not follow their advice. Therefore the onus is on the parents to give them godly guidance. Paul said to the Corinthians,

> *"Follow my example, as I follow the example of Christ."*
>
> — 1 CORINTHIANS 11:1

Paul did not ask us to follow his own man-made examples but of Christ. We, therefore, have no need of a university education to achieve godly parenting. All we need to do is to live by what Christ has taught us to be the best parent we can be. As King Solomon said,

> *"A righteous man who walks in his integrity – how blessed are his sons (and daughters) after him."*
>
> — PROVERBS 20:7

Parents are blamed for their children's misbehaviour, which largely results from neglect and lack of parent-child relationship. This, of course, becomes more apparent in single parents, who may have to work long hours in order to pay for every need of a home. Children growing up in homes where there is no good relationship between parents and children may suffer from emotional and behavioural problems that, if not dealt with effectively, may result in juvenile delinquency.

Parents need to take the blame if their children are out of hand. All children start off as being amenable to change. While children are young, parents have the opportunity to nurture them into well-behaved adults. Just like plants, if you expect your garden to look beautiful, you need to tend your flowers or vegetables, clear out weeds and feed them with good quality plant food. In like manner, and even much more, a child needs more than good food, beautiful clothes, good shoes, as well as a good house. He needs a warm, happy home, devoid of tension and violence. His growth should be all-round—physical, emotional, psychological and spiritual.

This growth does not come cheap. It requires a lifetime of hard work. It does not happen suddenly or overnight. A mango tree does not suddenly grow overnight. As big as it is, it starts off as a very small seed, planted in a well-watered soil, and it takes years to mature. You don't put it in the ground and turn your back, only to come back years later looking for fruits. There are 'enemies' all around—weeds, insects, birds, and animals—all wanting to take out your mango tree if you don't care. So your attention and care will let others know that you have not abandoned your plant.

Your children need more than all the above—they need your time, love, wealth, education, and influence. In fact, your *all* needs to be poured into raising your children to produce the best result. The earlier you start, the better the results. Training a child starts from pregnancy; God said, before the conception of Jeremiah, He already knew him and had given him a name. He says:

> *"Before I formed thee in the belly I knew thee; and before thou camest forth out of the womb I sanctified thee, and I ordained thee a prophet unto the nations."*

> — JEREMIAH 1:5

The same goes for all children. Children are part of God's creation and a heritage from Him, which He said was and is still good. When we reflect on the level of work God Himself did on Jeremiah before he was born, we will have an insight into what God expects each parent to do. It therefore follows that if children have the vital input for growth—spiritual, psychological and physical—they will achieve their God-given potential. That is why the Bible says:

"Train up a child in the way to go and when he grows up, he will not depart from it."

— PROVERBS 22:6

Whether we are aware of the passage of time or not, our children experience physical growth everyday and if not adequately nurtured will grow into unprepared adults with habits and attitudes that are difficult to drop later in life. Some might even have no good education that can earn them a decent living and while still coping with baggage from their youth, they suddenly realise they have become adults. As 'age' does not know whether you have resources to cope with your adulthood or not, 'adults' may want to marry or at least will be attracted to the opposite sex. A lack of sound foundation and preparedness may cause such moves to fail. Once people are of age, it is a natural phenomenon that a man may like to have a woman, and a woman may desire a man. It is not external knowledge acquired from college or by reading a book. It is part of the package at creation.

As a matter of fact, parents underestimate the rigour of training up children, otherwise, no one would have embarked on having children that will end up in the hands of just one of the parents. It is an abuse of nature as God designed it to be. If just one of the two parents can produce a child, or if one was enough to raise the child, God wouldn't have bothered to make them a pair of two. It goes without saying that leaving children in the hands of just one of the pair should not be thought of in the first place. No wonder the results are out there of children with one-sided upbringing, coping with forces greater than them.

When Father Abraham sent away Ishmael and his mother, all Hagar could do was to help him grow into "a wild man, free and untamed as a wild donkey, who lived at odds with his brethren" (Genesis 16:12). He had no role model in Abraham with a distance between them. He must have looked odd, living with a mum and no father in those days. All these events go to shape who children become in future. In fact, there are some children of single-parent who think less of themselves, feel inferior, insecure and see others as very unfriendly, to put it mildly.

The crucial question here is: **Is it possible for just a mother or a father to provide, effectively and efficiently, an environment in which a child or a number of children could thrive?**

PART ONE
GOD'S DIVINE PLAN FOR THE HOME

CHAPTER 1
GOD'S DESIGN FOR MARRIAGE AND FAMILY

> Joining together of a man and a woman is "an honourable estate, instituted by God in the time of man's innocence . . . adorned and beautified with His presence and first miracle that he wrought in Cana of Galilee." — p. 189, *Book of Common Prayer* (Reference: John 2:1-12)

One of the three reasons for the ordination of the Holy Matrimony is "the procreation of children, to be brought up in the fear and nurture of the Lord and to the praise of His holy Name." Therefore, every created being has two parents – be it human, animal, fish or bird. Biologically, no single parent can produce its like without the contribution of the 'opposite' other. This fact did not come clear on the fifth day of creation:

> **20** *Then God said, "Let the waters swarm with fish and other life. Let the skies be filled with birds of every kind."* **21** *So God created great sea creatures and every living thing that scurries and swarms in the water, and every sort of bird —each producing offspring of the same kind. And God saw that it was good.* **22** *Then God blessed them, saying, "Be fruitful and multiply. Let the fish fill the seas, and let the birds multiply on the earth."*
>
> **23** *And evening passed and morning came, marking the fifth day.*
>
> — GENESIS 1:20-23 NLT

However, for the sixth day:

> **24** *Then God said, "Let the earth produce every sort of animal, each producing offspring of the same kind—livestock, small animals that scurry along the ground, and wild animals." And that is what happened.* **25** *God made all sorts of wild animals, livestock, and small*

animals, each able to produce offspring of the same kind. And God saw that it was good.

26 *Then God said, "Let us make human beings in our image, to be like us. They will reign over the fish in the sea, the birds in the sky, the livestock, all the wild animals on the earth, and the small animals that scurry along the ground."*

27 *So God created human beings in his own image. In the image of God he created them; male and female he created them.*

— GENESIS 1:24-27 NLT

This gave us the knowledge that in order to reproduce, there must be male and female coming together. This is a divine command—

> ***28*** *Then God blessed them and said, "Be fruitful and multiply. Fill the earth and govern it. Reign over the fish in the sea, the birds in the sky, and all the animals that scurry along the ground." [i.e. have children and be master of everything]* . . . ***31*** *Then God looked over all he had made, and he saw that it was very good!*

And evening passed and morning came, marking the sixth day.

— GENESIS 1:28, 31 NLT

In the course of time,

> *5 The Lord observed the extent of human wickedness on the earth, and he saw that everything they thought or imagined was consistently and totally evil. 6 So the Lord was sorry he had ever made them and put them on the earth. It broke his heart. 7 And the Lord said, "I will wipe this human race I have created from the face of the earth. Yes, and I will destroy every living thing—all the people, the large animals, the small animals that scurry along the ground, and even the birds of the sky. I am sorry I ever made them." 8 But Noah found favor with the Lord.*

— GENESIS 6:5-8 NLT

In order to save Noah and his family from the imminent flood onslaught, God commanded him to build a boat, which would house Noah and his wife, his three sons and their three wives together with a pair (male and female) of every kind of animal.

This is so to maintain the continuity of existence; and all the remaining ones—be it human, animal and bird were wiped out by reason of the flood. In Genesis 2:5, we read that hitherto rain had never fallen upon the earth before the flood, the reason people disbelieved Noah and called him all sorts of names for obeying God. Therefore Noah's obedience saved him and his household. This is a lesson for a world that believes in 'the majority wins the vote' but not with God. Majority can be sincerely wrong and if we find ourselves in the minority but right with God, so be it.

> *5 So Noah did everything as the Lord commanded him.*
>
> *6 Noah was 600 years old when the flood covered the earth. 7 He went on board the boat to escape the flood—he and his wife and his sons and their wives. 8 With them were all the various kinds of animals—those approved for eating and for sacrifice and those that were not —along with all the birds and the small animals that scurry along the ground. 9 They entered the boat in pairs, male and female, just as God had commanded Noah. 10 After seven*

days, the waters of the flood came and covered the earth.

— GENESIS 7:5-10 NLT

Here God made it clear that to multiply, there needs to be a male and a female of the same kind coming together. If therefore, both have to come together to reproduce their kind, it is logical that the upbringing of that 'kind' should be the committed responsibility of both male and female if such a 'kind' is to grow into a well-balanced adult.

THINGS BEGAN TO FALL APART

The word of God in both the Old and New Testaments has not left us uninformed about what has brought about the fall of the family. Two references are discussed here.

First, in the Book of Malachi, it is written that:

> **14** *Yet you ask, Why does He reject it? Because the Lord was witness [to the covenant made at your marriage] between you and the wife of your youth, against whom you have dealt treacherously and to whom you were faithless. Yet she is your companion and the wife of your covenant [made by your marriage vows].*

***15** And did not God make [you and your wife] one [flesh]? Did not One make you and preserve your spirit alive? And why [did God make you two] one? Because He sought a godly offspring [from your union]. Therefore take heed to yourselves, and let no one deal treacherously and be faithless to the wife of his youth.*

***16** For the Lord, the God of Israel, says: I hate divorce and marital separation and him who covers his garment [his wife] with violence. Therefore keep a watch upon your spirit [that it may be controlled by My Spirit], that you deal not treacherously and faithlessly [with your marriage mate].*

— MALACHI 2:14-16 AMPC

The above Scriptures are the unchanging and unchangeable position of God and His Christ on the issue of marriage. This is where "procreation of children, to be brought up in the fear and nurture of the Lord and to the praise of His holy name" should take place. This is the light God has shone on this subject. The Word of God is light and is therefore not difficult to understand with the help of the Holy Spirit, who moves men and women of God to put down as they are instructed. Apostle Peter explains this clearly as follows:

> **20** *Knowing this first, that no prophecy of the scripture is of any private interpretation.*
>
> **21** *For the prophecy came not in old time by the will of man: but holy men of God spake as they were moved by the Holy Ghost.*
>
> — 2 PETER 1:20-21 KJV

As stated by Peter above, no word of God is of private interpretation which man can add to or subtract from and so becomes difficult to understand. As one preacher says:

> God means what He says and says what He means and He is not a joker.

In view of the above, we can safely say that single parenting is not God's idea and therefore made no provision for it in His holy Book, the Bible.

CHAPTER 2
WHY SINGLE PARENTING WAS NOT INTENDED BY GOD

Mary, a virgin, pregnant with a Baby by the Holy Spirit, had Joseph as her husband and earthly father to the unborn baby. How could a teenager be able to go through all we read about the early life of Jesus without the support of an able man? God, in all His omnipotence, still chose to provide a home for Jesus—He gave Jesus an earthly father and mother. Of course, God had and still has the power to drop Jesus from heaven as a fully grown man who needs no human support if He wished. He, however, did not do so to reiterate further His principle that a child should be cared for by his parents—and not by a *single* parent. It is not a surprise, therefore, that God made no provision for single parenting in His Word, the Bible, because single parenting was not and is still not His idea.

The Bible says,

> *"Even if everyone else is a liar, God is true"*
> *because "he cannot deny who he is"*
>
> — ROMANS 3:4 NLT; 2 TIMOTHY 2:13 NLT

Therefore, when Joseph, "a just man," was about to call off his marriage with Mary, the angel of God appeared to him to brief him about God's plan, as follows:

> ***19*** *Then Joseph her husband, being a just man, and not willing to make her a publick example, was minded to put her away privily.* ***20*** *But while he thought on these things, behold, the angel of the Lord appeared unto him in a dream, saying, Joseph, thou son of David, fear not to take unto thee Mary thy wife: for that which is conceived in her is of the Holy Ghost.*
>
> — MATTHEW 1:19-20 KJV

A girl "found with child" was an abomination in those days. That was how God's people held in high esteem the institution of marriage in Bible times. We recall the story of Judah and Tamar in Genesis 38. Tamar deceived Judah

WHY SINGLE PARENTING WAS NOT INTENDED BY GO... • 13

in revenge for his own deceit because Judah refused his son, Shelah, to marry her. She pretended to be a harlot instead of a widow, and Judah went in to her. This resulted in the pregnancy of a set of twin boys. When Judah was told that his late son's wife was pregnant, he was swift to pronounce a death sentence on her because he thought she had brought shame on his family by becoming pregnant without a legitimate husband.

> **24** *And it came to pass about three months after, that it was told Judah, saying, Tamar thy daughter in law hath played the harlot; and also, behold, she is with child by whoredom. And Judah said, Bring her forth, and let her be burnt.*
>
> — GENESIS 38:24 KJV

But for the evidence provided by Tamar that Judah was actually responsible for the pregnancy, having waited endlessly for a member of the family to inherit her after her husband's death, she would have been put to death.

However in the case of Joseph, a just man, he was not willing to disgrace Mary, so he chose to end the engagement secretly. His merciful attitude gives an insight into his true nature as a man, which, by the mercy of God, qualifies him to be called the father of Jesus. Let us relish more on the godly character of Joseph, who had no knowledge of the father of Mary's baby and yet was willing to spare her the ridicule and the probable public execution that might befall her as well as take on the punishment with her. Since there was no man to point to, he might have well be accused of adultery with Mary!

I read, some years ago, a book titled *Windows on Christmas*, written by Bill Crowder, one of the writers of *Our Daily Bread*. This beautiful book is essentially about the different 'actors' involved in the miraculous birth of Jesus. Joseph, His mother's would-be husband, happened to be one of them. What was of great interest to me is the way the author likened Joseph to a man who became a stepfather "he didn't have to be," but "chose" to become anyway.

The story is about a single mom of an only boy who found it difficult to have a stable relationship because of the young boy until, one day, a particular man turned up. Hitherto, men pulled back as soon as they knew the lady had a little boy. However, when this man called to take this boy's mom out, he willingly invited the boy to come along, and a bond of friendship developed between them. The story concluded with a scene whereby the little boy had become a father, too. The author writes,

WHY SINGLE PARENTING WAS NOT INTENDED BY GO... • 15

> Now married himself, the young man stands outside the observation window of a hospital nursery looking at his own new-born baby, with his stepfather at his side. His longing and desire and prayer? That he will be able to be half the dad his stepfather "didn't have to be."

We are talking about choices here.

> The man he had grown to love as his father could have turned around and walked away. He had a choice, and he chose to be a dad. He chose to be what he didn't have to be. He chose to love.

Joseph, the husband of Mary, is like the man described above in many ways. He had choices to make even though God sent an angel to deliver the message to him. There are people in the Bible whom God had called upon to do one thing or the other but refused, complained, grumbled and even ran away, but not Joseph. He obeyed just like Father Abraham, who was asked to embark on a journey, not knowing where he was going. Joseph set out on an unknown life journey. He had only the message from God as a road map and a compass. No one had ever plied the road before him or after him, so there was no experience to call upon.

As God will never contradict Himself, He arranged that Jesus should be born and brought up in a proper home, raised by a husband and a wife. Apostle Paul told us in many places that all the events that happened and are recorded in the Bible are not for fun or mere storytelling but for our examples to follow.

> "Now all these things happened unto them for examples: and they are written for our admonition, upon whom the ends of the world are come."
>
> — 1 CORINTHIANS 10:11 KJV

The people of old had no such privileges of "examples to follow," yet Noah, Abraham and Joseph chose to obey.

THE CASE FOR INEVITABLE SINGLE PARENTING

In light of what had been said about God's ideal for parenting being with a father and a mother raising their children together, there seems to be an unanswered question. The truth is that not every single parenting is an act of disobedience. When sin entered into the world shortly after creation, it brought with it death, as Apostle said in his epistle to the Romans,

> *"Wherefore, as by one man sin entered into the world, and death by sin; and so death passed upon all men, for that all have sinned."*

— ROMANS 5:12 KJV

Therefore, that all will die physically is a settled matter. However, the timing is very crucial. Everyone wishes to grow into old age when dependants would be mature enough to take care of themselves. If God's stance above is non-negotiable, what happens when the unavoidable occurs? What happens in the case of the premature death of one of the parents or even both?

In Exodus 22:22-24, God Himself says:

> *"Ye shall not afflict any widow, or fatherless child. If thou afflict them in any wise, and they cry at all unto me, I will surely hear their cry; And my wrath shall wax hot, and I will kill you with the sword; and your wives shall be widows, and your children fatherless."*

— EXODUS 22:22-24 KJV

The above is a very fearful statement. If God is ready to avenge such treatment of the widow and her children, we cannot begin to imagine His reaction when we decide to substitute His instructions.

In 2 Kings 4, during the time of Elisha, a widow cried out for help to rescue her two sons from their creditor. Elisha responded immediately, and a miracle happened, and the widow's sons were saved from becoming slaves to the creditor. In Luke 7:11-15, Jesus also had compassion on a widow whose only son died by bringing him back to life, and the passage ends by emphasising, "and she was a widow."

In our day-to-day encounter with the world, widows are likely to be attended to on more compassionate grounds than a single parent. Conversely, rather than helping single parents, they are, more often than not, taken advantage of, as a result of their vulnerable condition.

CHAPTER 3
SINGLE PARENTHOOD IN HISTORICAL CONTEXT

There was a time when it was defiant to become a single parent. Back then, the society saw it as an affront. Once married, most women stayed married whatever befell them. This was so because in those days the majority of women, if not all, had no means of livelihood. Their dependence, therefore, was on their husbands. So becoming a single parent could be described as the worst situation a woman would opt to be in. It was a life journey plagued with uncertainty, fear, danger, hatred, mockery, isolation, or even death. Indeed, the list of possible challenges that would attend such a reality is endless. If an unmarried lady became pregnant, she became an object of ridicule among her peers, both boys and girls. It is not uncommon that the perpetrator, who might even be her would-be husband, could deny and join others in making life miserable for her. And since DNA testing was not yet available back then, there was no way to identify the father of an unborn child. Such a lady would become isolated even within her father's house for bringing shame upon her family. Therefore, ladies did not dare to lose their virginity, not even to their would-be husbands; else they would live in disgrace for the rest of their lives. They were constantly at the mercy of the other women, making their life miserable both at home and in the community. They became a laughing stock. It was a stigma in those days even on the child who knew nothing about the whole scenario that brought him or her to life.

As earlier mentioned, the position of the Bible is more severe on the above issue. Moses, in Deuteronomy 22:13-30, gave the Israelites six laws of chastity as being foundational to family integrity. Punishments for violating the laws varied:

> *13 If any man take a wife, and go in unto her, and hate her, 14 And give occasions of speech against her, and bring up an evil name upon her, and say, I took this woman, and when I came to her, I found her not a maid: 15 Then shall the father of the damsel, and her mother,*

*take and bring forth the tokens of the damsel's virginity unto the elders of the city in the gate: **16** And the damsel's father shall say unto the elders, I gave my daughter unto this man to wife, and he hateth her; **17** And, lo, he hath given occasions of speech against her, saying, I found not thy daughter a maid; and yet these are the tokens of my daughter's virginity. And they shall spread the cloth before the elders of the city. **18** And the elders of that city shall take that man and chastise him; **19** And they shall amerce him in an hundred shekels of silver, and give them unto the father of the damsel, because he hath brought up an evil name upon a virgin of Israel: and she shall be his wife; he may not put her away all his days. **20** But if this thing be true, and the tokens of virginity be not found for the damsel: **21** Then they shall bring out the damsel to the door of her father's house, and the men of her city shall stone her with stones that she die: because she hath wrought folly in Israel, to play the whore in her father's house: so shalt thou put evil away from among you."*

— DEUTERONOMY 22:13-21 KJV

The punishment was so severe that others, especially women, would see it and avoid adultery, as they would pay with their lives. From generation to generation, women have often been blamed more than men for cooperating with men in their lustfulness, without considering the strength and threat employed by men against women. While some women might be guilty indeed, that is no reason for the men to be exonerated, as one renowned preacher said, "both of them should be blamed and punished."

> ***22** If a man be found lying with a woman married to an husband, then they shall both of them die, both the man that lay with the woman, and the woman: so shalt thou put away evil from Israel.*
>
> ***23** If a damsel that is a virgin be betrothed unto an husband, and a man find her in the city, and lie with her;*
>
> ***24** Then ye shall bring them both out unto the gate of that city, and ye shall stone them with stones that they die; the damsel, because she cried not, being in the city; and the man, because he hath humbled his neighbour's wife: so thou shalt put away evil from among you.*

***25** But if a man find a betrothed damsel in the field, and the man force her, and lie with her: then the man only that lay with her shall die:*

***26** But unto the damsel thou shalt do nothing; there is in the damsel no sin worthy of death: for as when a man riseth against his neighbour, and slayeth him, even so is this matter:*

***27** For he found her in the field, and the betrothed damsel cried, and there was none to save her.*

***28** If a man find a damsel that is a virgin, which is not betrothed, and lay hold on her, and lie with her, and they be found;*

***29** Then the man that lay with her shall give unto the damsel's father fifty shekels of silver, and she shall be his wife; because he hath humbled her, he may not put her away all his days."*

— DEUTERONOMY 22:22-29 KJV

The last verse in that chapter was not one of the laws but is very relevant to the stability of the family:

> *"A man shall not take his father's wife, nor discover his father's skirt."*
>
> — DEUTERONOMY 22:30 KJV

The above statement is an instruction which has no punishment attached. However, Reuben was known in the Bible to have violated the instruction and lost his firstborn right to Joseph as his punishment (Genesis 35:22). Another culprit was Absalom, who went into his father's concubines as an act of rebellion against King David. Absalom was killed in the ensuing battle between him and his father (2 Kings 18).

In Psalm 19, the psalmist says:

> *"The law of the Lord is perfect, converting the soul; the testimony of the Lord is sure, making wise the simple. The statutes of the Lord are right, rejoicing the heart: the commandment of the Lord is pure, enlightening the eyes. The fear of the Lord is clean, enduring forever: the judgments of the Lord are true and righteous altogether. More to be desired are they than gold, yea, than much fine gold: sweeter also than honey and the honeycomb. Moreover by them is*

thy servant warned: and in keeping of them there is great reward."

— PSALM 19:7-11 KJV

Every law of God is for our benefit, and its violation carries consequences. The above psalm says many things: we are to love everything in the law of God more than gold or honey, for in them we have a great reward. However, there are warnings therein, too, and failure to comply attracts penalties, some of which are very harsh.

Let us consider 'the great reward'. If we build our homes on the law of God, we have everything we need because the law of God serves as a conduit through which all other issues of life are channelled. It helps in giving consideration to every situation. It is a teacher and an adviser on every issue. It is a guide as well as a mirror.

When we make the law of God our focus, each person ends up doing what the other is doing, for we both drink from the same source—the law of God. We know who God is through His law, faithful and very impartial in all His ways. If only we operate the same rules and regulations, no one will be in doubt as to what is right or wrong. There would be love as well as order, peace, stability and understanding in the home.

Conversely, when anyone decides to bend the rules to satisfy their selfishness and greed, chaos, confusion, suspicion, and the like will be their portion. Indeed, if not curtailed, it may lead to untold hardship both for the perpetrators and for everyone in their path.

Therefore, the laws of God are very good for us, and they are not grievous; rather, they are easy to understand. According to Apostle Peter, the law of God is not of any "private interpretation." We therefore have no excuse.

Whether we like it or not, believe it or not, flouting the above laws and instructions is the bedrock of the numerous dysfunctional homes in our society today. One preacher says: "At the root of every human crisis are ungodliness and unrighteousness." The crisis we hear or watch on TV or witness live on our streets—they all have their root-cause in the homes. Violence that was hitherto shown in films in the past has become live occurrences on the TV every day. Technology has denied us the peace people enjoyed in those days when we only read of calamities which had happened months ago in the newspapers. In fact many of these events were never reported. As a result, their ferocity was never felt in far away areas of the world. The same cannot be said of the world we live in now. The prayer of the psalmist in Psalm 91:5-6 is a prayer we must pray 24/7:

> *'Thou shalt not be afraid for the terror by night; nor for the arrow that flieth by day; Nor for the pestilence that walketh in darkness; nor for the destruction that wasteth at noonday.'*
>
> — PSALM 91:5-6 KJV

Take, for instance, the 9/11 disaster in which, within minutes, the twin towers were razed down in New York in broad daylight. It looked like fiction as people watching thought it was a new film. The whole picture was captured vividly by cameras of many media organisations as if they were waiting for it to happen. Another horrible episode was the shooting of miners by the police in South Africa in 2012 where 37 were dead within minutes—also on a sunny day. Cameras were also waiting. Calamities like these happen because the home has lost its rightful place on Earth. It is unimaginable that young men and women could engage themselves in such horrendous missions, except that homes have failed to produce godly children by showing them the way of peace.

As far as we know from the scriptures, the God-ordained way to have and raise children is between married God-fearing couples. This is not to say that all their children are brought up accordingly or that there will not be disobedient ones among them. However, if two-parent couples experience difficulties and challenges in bringing up their children, it goes without saying that single parents will experience much more upheaval. This is principally as a result of one person doing the work of two.

In a comprehensive study conducted by Bebbington and Miles (1989),[1] they compared two-parent households to single-parent households in developed countries. Their findings revealed that a child who grows up in a family with both parents, without relying on benefits, residing in a household with three or fewer children, situated in a larger owner-occupied residence, and being of white ethnicity, has an extremely low likelihood of being placed in foster care – just 1 in 7,000 odds. Conversely, a child from a larger family, raised by a single parent, dependent on benefits, coming from a mixed ethnic background, and living in an overcrowded privately-rented dwelling, particularly in a deprived neighbourhood, faces a significantly higher chance of entering foster care – a 1 in 10 chance.

That the children of single parents are more likely to end up with social service than those of two parents is not borne out of malice or prejudice. The reality is that the statement is factual that no one person can do the work of two people effectively and efficiently, however strong and determined they may be.

1. BEBBINGTON, ANDREW, and JOHN MILES. "The Background of Children Who Enter Local Authority Care." *The British Journal of Social Work* 19, no. 5 (1989): 349–68. http://www.jstor.org/stable/23708819.

CHAPTER 4
DIVERSE PATHWAYS INTO SINGLE PARENTHOOD

Single parenting results from various circumstances. We will consider some of them in this chapter.

DEATH OF ONE PARENT

The death of one of the parents accounts for an unavoidable single-parenting situation, as earlier mentioned. God has, however, taken up their care.

UNPLANNED PREGNANCIES

Unwanted and/or unplanned pregnancies that occur in unmarried teenage girls could also result in single parenting. These pregnancies come along unexpectedly, usually when young boys and girls of the same age bracket engage in sexual union. In some cases, the boy may deny having an affair with the girl and may even take to their heels. Unless the girl's parents are magnanimous enough to keep the baby while the mother returns to school, their education may be grounded to a halt or, at times, that may be the end of it. Such girls are without qualifications and therefore usually unemployable.

If thrown out by their parents, they become homeless and endangered. Before long, they become pregnant again, and history repeats itself. The resultant outcome is that such girls may have as many as four kids from different fathers. As could be expected, a great percentage of children taken into care in countries where social services exist come from teenage girls.

Unmarried mature mothers now have scientific means of having children without necessarily involving themselves in any man's home. Most decide to have one or two kids. However, some of them still have children through married men or divorcees and widowers with children.

This is an arena for conflict, especially with the wives of the married men, and if the children of the divorcees and widowers are grown-ups, there is bound to be protests. Well-off single mothers will probably not involve themselves and their children in any conflict with the affected families. After all, to them, what they need are children, and they have everything to cater for them. However, this may not be taken lightly by the families who see themselves as having been cheated by their fathers. Neither have such arrangements been smooth sailing ever from the time the world began. We have the extreme case of Gideon in Judges 8 and 9, where his son Abimelech by his concubine went to Gideon's house at Ophrah and killed all his seventy sons except the youngest, who escaped.

UNEXPECTED SEPARATIONS

The last category of single parenting occurs through separation or divorce and is the most daunting of single parenting — 2 people, married with children within their wedlock and later separated or divorced. This is a most devastating situation. Their own condition could be likened to a tree uprooted and left to survive without water. In some cultures, it is the woman that is thrown out, in others, the man simply takes his suitcase and departs. In either case, the effect is the same. A woman who decides to leave will be homeless; adding her children to that condition will be nothing less than catastrophic. In the second and third categories stated above, there had never been a two-parent family. The children had always known one parent, or, at best, the other has been a visitor —if they come at all.

In the last category, the children had been living with both parents all their life until the separation. So, two parents becoming one overnight, besides having to pack out to some unfamiliar neighbourhood can be devastating and destabilising. To call it a shattered life is an understatement. No word is capable of summing it up. While the woman may have her strong reasons for leaving, the truth is that as reality settles in, she will begin to see the future as bleak, confused, chaotic and unimaginable. The obstacles on the road to survival are huge and numerous.

SINGLE PARENTING WITHIN HOMES

There is a rare group of women who are married but could become a single parent for one reason or the other.

Polygamous Dynamics

Most of the wives of Gideon could be described as single parents for the simple reason that they must be many to have given him seventy sons without counting the girls. It is therefore not possible for one man to be a devoted husband to any of the women. The same goes with Solomon who had seven hundred wives. If any of the women in such a situation failed to take full responsibility for bringing up her children, she would have missed the point.

When Abraham and Sarah had no child, Sarah gave her slave girl, Hagar, to her husband to raise a male child for them. What a thought, as well as an assumption! Sarah must have overestimated her claim of ownership over her slave as to believe that the child produced by Hagar would belong to her. Of course, she was disappointed! A woman is a woman, whether behind the mill or seated on a throne. Sarah soon found out that she had made the most devastating error of her life, and so remained childless for a season, while Abraham and Hagar were head over heels about *their* son. However, at the appointed time, God remembered Sarah in her anguish and gave her the promised son. It was an amazing, unbelievable, and inconceivable reality. Hagar must have been thrown into panic when that happened, because, from then on, Ishmael became *Hagar's* son. Eventually, she was sent packing and became entirely responsible for Ishmael's upbringing afterwards. After Sarah died, Abraham married again and had six other boys, and the scenario plays out again.

The Solitude of Childless Wives

Hannah, the mother of Prophet Samuel, is another striking example. She was a single parent while waiting on

God for Samuel as her husband had another wife who bore him many children.

Rachel, Jacob's favourite wife, found it difficult to get pregnant in time. She was very angry with her husband and also became jealous of her sister. At one point, Jacob became frustrated and retorted that he could not take the place of God when Rachel demanded that he should give her a child. Jacob loved her so much but not to the point of being able to give her a child, and so, in a sense, she was a single parent looking up to God for a child. At this juncture, Jacob already had 10 sons!

The Unwavering Bond of Motherhood

Many women also become single parents on their children's 'bad days.' For instance, a Yoruba adage says, *"Ọmọ tó bá dáa ni ti baba, èyí tí kò bá dáa ni ti ìyá,"* meaning *"A good child belongs to the father, whereas the bad child belongs to the mother."* Mothers travel across oceans to rescue their children. In times of trouble—whether facing a jail term, sickness, or loss—mothers will not be found wanting. It is not easy for a woman to disown her troublesome child. At such difficult times, most mothers become single parents and are ready to take the place of their children.

Zebedee's sons, John and James, were taken to Jesus by their mother and requested that Jesus would let them sit one on His right and the other on His left in His kingdom. She did not even ask for herself! Hers was a selfish ambition. The apostles of Jesus were twelve. However, this woman did not bother herself about democracy or equality but made up her mind to 'take the Kingdom of God by force'. Incidentally, Jesus never queried her for asking Him for the best positions for her sons. Women singularly go out to seek the best for their children.

The above scenarios indicate that nearly all women become single parents while waiting for a child, seeking the best for their children or in time of trouble.

CHAPTER 5
SINGLE PARENTING AND THE SOCIETY

SOCIETAL ATTITUDES AND THE EMOTIONAL LANDSCAPE OF SINGLE PARENTING

As stated before, single parenting is a life journey plagued with uncertainty, fear, danger, hatred, mockery, isolation or even death, the list is endless. In the past, society had a zero-tolerance approach to single parenting for very good reasons as stated in Chapter 3 and therefore worked very hard to discourage it. In some cultures, single mothers experience barriers in almost all departments of life. People take advantage of them because of their situation. They can be cheated, knowing that they have no one to defend them.

Single mothers are not welcomed in many communities, especially in the more civilised societies where like-minded people live together. Other married women would gang up to oust a single mother from their midst. There is no sympathy towards her. Women are naturally blamed for their single-parenthood even by other women, and so life might become difficult for them. Some relocate to a totally new place in order to have a fresh start.

At the beginning, it could be frightening to realise that you are now alone with your children. There would be feelings of fear, anger, frustration, doubt, guilt, abandonment, confusion, loneliness and many more. These feelings depend very much on why and how your situation came about. The truth of the matter is, if you are fleeing from violence, your first reaction might be relief. Being alone in your home with your children shouldn't make you lonely and helpless. The reality is that the task before you is enormous and cannot be handled by you alone. You need the support of friends and relations. Don't overestimate your strength; rather acknowledge the task before you. You will then be able to plan the way forward and how to live your life from that moment onwards.

THE ROLE OF SOCIAL SERVICES IN DEVELOPED COUNTRIES

For the benefit of those who have no 'social services' as practised in the developed world, there is a need for an insight into the work of social services regarding single parents and their children. In the developed world, a mother may be breaking the law if she leaves her children under the age of 12 alone in the house, even if it is just to buy bread from the corner shop. The children are likely to be taken away by law enforcement agents before she returns. This point explains why most single parents are not working when their children are still young, which is alien to mothers in other less developed nations of the world. For those in the developed world, the state renders financial support for the upkeep of the children. The state has taken steps—in good faith, I believe—so that the children might develop into responsible adults of the future.

Admittedly, in a welfare state, single mothers are given allowances to care for their kids. However, raising them needs much more than allowances to make them successful in life. Love and attention are very vital to their development. However much a mother of four kids likes to love and be attentive, it is impracticable when two or three need immediate attention, especially on health grounds. The situation of the younger parents is more precarious than that of the older for lack of education, viable jobs and experience.

UNIQUE STRUGGLES OF YOUNG SINGLE PARENTS

Largely in developing countries, closely-knit communities still exist where next-door neighbours could be relations or older women who could assist working mothers in caring for infants while they are at work. This practice seems non-existent in industrialised countries with fragmented communities. Adult children have moved away from their parents in search of jobs in cities and, therefore, could not be assisted by their parents or relations. This is a major concern for single women who want to work, especially if they are well-educated. They either stay home until their young ones are of school age, or pay huge amounts to nurseries to keep the kids for them during office hours. Those without qualifications to work find themselves stuck in the house. This accounts, in part, for the poverty, which is characteristic of young and out-of-job single parents.

EMBRACING NEW WORK MODELS IN SINGLE PARENTHOOD

Becoming a single parent could be very daunting for a working person. It is an embarrassing situation, and others are bound to gossip. You may even find it shameful to turn up at your office the next day. However, whether they understand or not, you have to move on with your life. Your state of mind is crucial here. In order not to jeopardise your career, you can decide to take a break from work to sort yourself out, provided you have other sources of funds to cater for your needs during your break, like savings or dividends from investments, etc. If however, you have nothing to fall back to, and you have to keep on working, you can then take some time off (like a holiday) during which you can sort out a lot of issues and get some rest also. You need to demonstrate to your employers that what has happened to you will not, in any way, damage your work/career. If you have been an efficient worker before, chances are that your employers will support you to overcome your stressful period.

In the developed world, there are many variables to working hours. You can work part-time in some jobs. People work from home in this technological age, and even conferences are conducted via video links. Depending on your special training and discipline, you may be in a position to start your own businesses, which you can run from home.

CHAPTER 6
THE CRUCIAL INTERPLAY OF FATHER AND MOTHER IN A WELL-BALANCED HOME
THE BODY ANALOGY

THE DYNAMICS OF A BALANCED HOME

A home is a body of two principal parts: a father and a mother. The home cannot function well with just one part, both are needed to create a well-balanced home. Each part has its own unique responsibility which completes and complements the other part. Their functions are not the same, just as Apostle Paul says,

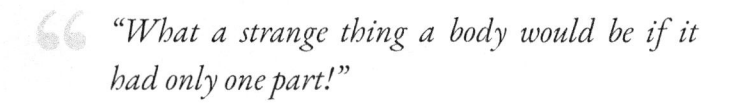

> *"What a strange thing a body would be if it had only one part!"*
>
> — 1 CORINTHIANS 12:19 NIV

The same thing applies to a home where there is only a part of the body making up a home. It is quite strange for any of the two to say, "I don't need the other part," or just because it is not the other part, it is not a part of the body. That one part is not sufficient enough to make the whole body does not make it less a part of the body. Paul gave this powerful analogy to demonstrate God's wisdom at creation — He created them male and female for life, to do God's work and to be ready to give account on the Day of Judgment.

It goes without saying that when a part is missing, the job is half done and ends in dysfunctional results. Children need both parts of the home-body in order to be who God wants them to be. Tragically, we tend to forget this fact and so dismiss those who are different from us. Whereas, if we accept each other as God has accepted and forgiven us, the home, and the world, by extension, would be a better place today, as a greater percentage of the world's trouble stems from the rejection of others who are not our 'type' or 'kind'.

SINGLE PARENTING: A CHALLENGE COMPARABLE TO DISABILITY

Some parts of the body come in pairs—left and right. In other words, they don't necessarily stay together but are arranged in a way that balances the whole body. Examples are ears, eyes, arms, legs, kidneys, lungs and ovaries. Each pair does the same work effectively. However, in the event of a loss of one part of the pair, the function becomes the responsibility of the remaining one. This situation often leads to over-work and eventual breakdown. Where there is no breakdown, their function takes longer than usual to carry out, as they become less efficient and clumsy. On the other hand, just half of a pair is incapable of its function. While an eye can see, an arm cannot lift a heavy bag up without help. The same goes with one leg. It is not possible for just one leg to move the body around without aid. People with such disabilities find it difficult to be employed and are denied many privileges which able-bodied people take for granted.

Placed side by side with the above scenario, single-parenting is a sort of *disability*. The roles in a home are diverse and enormous, most of which go on simultaneously. Even two people struggle to cope at times, let alone one.

Let us examine a typical day in the life of a family of two working parents with two or three kids under the age of seven, who have to be delivered to their school/nursery every morning before the parents head for work. It is noteworthy that the success of the next day is enhanced by its preparation the previous night. The adage "early to bed, early to rise" comes into play here. Young children, who are to rise up as early as 6 am to get ready for school, must retire to bed by 9 pm if they are to be fully rested. Each morning, preparation goes on in two major areas: getting the children ready for school and cooking of meals—breakfast and lunch. Lunch could be optional as the couple could eat lunch out. Therefore, all hands will be on deck every morning in order to leave home on time.

Thanks to schools and their able teachers who take charge from 8 am to 3.30 pm; however, most working-class parents close at 5 pm, which leaves a space of two hours to be filled. Again, thanks to "After-School Centres," which help to keep children of working-couples. Some contingencies have been left out like distances between home and school, and between school and places of work. Nevertheless, they are important to the overall success of each day. Another factor that should be taken into consideration has to do with couples working in different workplaces but having only one means of transport. It goes without saying that additional time will be needed to cope with such logistics. There are cases where couples have no means of private transport and therefore rely on public transport over which they have no control. It is no exaggeration to say that the above situation will be hectic for two people and extremely difficult for just one person. If things sometimes go wrong with couples, be sure that it might be worse with single parents.

RISKS AND VULNERABILITIES OF SINGLE PARENTING

Over the years, some single parents (women) have been murdered either by ex-husbands or present partners. In some cases, the children have suffered the same fate. Not too long ago, a lady killed her two lovely, well-looked after children because the situation became unbearable for her, having to take care of them and at the same time working. She became so mentally stressed to the point that she took the lives of her own children. Another lady was killed along with her two adult children by her partner. Reports say that she was a hard-working woman as well as her two children who have already gained admission to the University. Some toddlers have been brutally killed by both their mothers and current partners because the poor kids were getting in the way. The list goes on and on. The fact of the matter is that not all these women enjoy their situation.

PART TWO
PRACTICAL INSIGHTS FOR SINGLE PARENTS

CHAPTER 7

NAVIGATING YOUR NEW REALITY AND FAMILY DYNAMICS IN SINGLE PARENTHOOD

ADJUSTING TO YOUR NEW SITUATION

Adjusting to your new situation might take some time, so be patient with your children and yourself. You need to be strong and healthy to avoid a complete collapse of your set-up. Some women might lose their mind and suffer a breakdown which may lead to their children being taken into foster care. Where a society has no foster care system, families and friends might have to take up the care of the children—an arrangement that might not last or be sustainable.

REORGANISING YOUR HOME

The organisation of tasks is crucial to running a home successfully. Avoid piling up tasks. Share chores according to the ages and capabilities of the children so that everyone will have something to do—even the youngest should be capable of putting away the toys scattered all over the place. You need to develop a routine and a rota. Every member should know what to do at any given time. This will enhance early retirement every evening. Haphazard or shoddy arrangement only leads to chaos and frustration.

MANAGING YOUR LIVING SPACE AND MORTGAGE CONSIDERATIONS

If you have been living in your own house before, your ex might have been responsible for the maintenance and repairs of your home. Now, as a woman, you may have to move out, as some cultures demand, in a separation. If you have no house of your own, it means you will have to rent an apartment.

As a woman, if you already have a home of your own and your ex leaves, you need to decide whether to keep the house or not, especially if your ex refuses to continue paying the mortgage. You need not over-stretch your finances at this stage. If he is still willing to pay the mortgage, fine. However, you may be responsible for any repairs to the house from now on. You can take out home insurance where it exists and thereby save yourself the task of handling repairs when needed. However, it will cost you a regular contribution to an insurance company.

If you have to change location, consider the area very well, especially in relation to your children. At least, the standard ought to be the same or even higher than where you are coming from. Distance to your children's schools is also important. If possible, you can move nearer to your place of work as well. Distances to your place of work and your children's schools from your home are so crucial that they need to be minimised to relieve you of the stress of travelling several miles every day. In all these, the standard of the schools should be paramount.

NAVIGATING FINANCIAL CHALLENGES

How to survive on just one salary could be worrisome where it two salaries have always been used in running the home. The situation here is quite individualistic. For those whose ex-partners have been generous, they need to adjust their style of spending. However, for those who spend all their earnings on the home with little or nothing coming from their ex, only a little adjustment will be needed. They are already used to it. If however, you realise that your earnings cannot cope with your needs, you have to readjust your spending in the interim. There are many ways of doing this without necessarily compromising your standard of living. The first thing to do is to cut off wastage, which exists in every home as well as reduce excesses.

You may have to look for a better-paying job or improve your qualifications to earn a promotion. In the immediate, your family members might be willing to help you settle down, though they may not be in favour of your decision to become solely responsible for your children.

It is pertinent to say that money matters and should not be mixed up with what or who caused the separation. Without adequate finance, the day-to-day existence of a home might be in jeopardy. Financing the home is the collective responsibility of both parents. It is only fair that the absentee parent should realise that if one parent takes on all the running around for their children, it goes without saying that they should contribute more generously towards the upkeep of their children. When this is not forthcoming, your children will suffer. Some absentee parents starve their own children of finance as a sort of punishment for the resident parent.

It is unthinkable to see parents refusing to cater for their children for any reason at all. It is unimaginable! The care of the children should not be compromised. If care is not taken and the children get to know about the situation, it can result in emotional disturbance. Before you know it, they can begin to show traces of insecurity at school or even bad behaviour.

Both parents, whether they live together or not, are responsible for the well-being of their children on all fronts, finance inclusive. It is a shame that parents should be selective on what they can do for their children for any reason at all. Whatever the weather, the children remain theirs. It is an understatement to say that money plays a crucial role in our existence. A lot of damage has been done and is still being experienced by children who are starved of funds during their childhood years. Such children are not likely to attain their God-given potential, and some could become criminals in an attempt to make ends meet.

It is remarkable to note that money has always played a significant role in conflicts that eventually led to the break-up of many homes simply because one party blatantly decided to cheat the other party. The one cheating often uses force and threats to bring their victim to submission. This situation may eventually break the relationship. It is no wonder, therefore, that when the end comes to their union, the issue of money continues to dominate their future relationship.

Some of the absentee parents in countries with social services, where the government assists parents with children's maintenance allowance, rely solely on such money without adding to it! Such parents should be asked what relationship or link remains between them and their children now that the government is in charge.

It looks absurd to refuse to give to your own kids what you willingly give to your relations or even those not related to you. At the end of the day, you are left with your own. However much you are loved because you have lavished your wealth on them, they can never be called your children. Your children need you and your substance the most, now that they are growing up. It is the most critical and delicate part of their life, whereby any mistake made is possible to change their course of life forever.

CHANGING SOCIAL CIRCLES AND FRIENDSHIPS

Like begets like. Couples flow with each other. Becoming single may lead to a disintegration of established friendships, usually into three camps: yours, his/hers and neither of yours. This is not to say you are at fault. However, traditionally, couples have little in common with single parents, even in churches. This is so because you, as a single parent, have limited time for social gatherings because of the huge task at home. On the other hand, most of those events invite couples and singles alike, but most couples-turned-singles decline such invitations for obvious reasons. In all these, singles should not begrudge couples or even take it out on themselves. What you need is time and space to come to terms with the new status.

Often spouses, especially men, discourage their wives from keeping relationships with friends who are now separated from their husbands. They fear their wives could be influenced into doing the same. Women, too, could become afraid that their husbands may be attracted to their friends. Children of single parents may also suffer the loss of former friends who are children of their parents' friends. Such parents discourage their kids from continuing their friendship.

This could be very damaging to children of now single parents. One thing is clear, you can't change people overnight; however, you can change your own perspective by seeing things positively rather than negatively and in no distant time, people will begin to realign with your way of life.

Help your children to choose their friends, not by dictating who to choose but by supporting them to choose right. However, if they want to choose those you would rather not want them to choose, you need understanding as well as a lot of prayers and patience to let them see your point of view. You need to listen more to them rather than enforcing your will, which may be counter-productive.

MANAGING FAMILY SUPPORT

Your family members may have no choice but to support you since you belong to them come rain and sunshine, though not all will agree with your decision. However, their support should not include putting down your children or their other parent. This attitude does not augur well for you, your children or even your ex and their own relations. All should remember that whatever happens, families remain forever, even if they do not see eye to eye. It is not impossible that as generations come and go, some members might discover themselves in future and become friends; therefore no parting or separation should be taken as absolute.

Grandparents on both sides can be helpful. Yours can be a natural relationship. However, your ex's parents and relations may or may not be friendly towards you. They might have been on a warring path with you during your marriage, and the split might be welcoming to them. So befriending you and your children can be hard work for them. Such grandparents never see their son/daughter in their grandchildren. The situation may be short-lived, especially if your kids are grown up. They have the right to make up their mind by showing love towards their grandparents, and a relationship can evolve.

ENTERING THE DATING SCENE AGAIN

Thinking of dating and getting into another relationship requires a lot of hard work, especially if you have children to consider or your would-be partner has children too. Your age and that of your children will play a crucial role in your decision. If you are young, you may want to remarry. However, if you have had enough children to look after, that is another dimension to your situation. The same goes for the person you will want to marry. Your situation will determine what you do. There are no two identical situations, so you have no one to copy, and it is never a cut-and-dried situation. You have your rights to exercise as well as needs to be met, albeit within the framework of your peculiar situation. It is advisable that whatever decision you make, it should impact positively on everyone concerned.

You need to retrain yourself in the art of dating and building new relationships. Your former relationship should be put behind you firmly if the new one is to succeed. It is not uncommon for people to experience conflict between the two relationships. The truth is, there are so many issues to settle before and during the new relationship, which, if brushed aside, may come back to disrupt the new setting. There are also many people involved, whether dead or alive. If both of you are winding up old relationships to pave way for the new one, you cannot wind up your relations on both sides, except there are no children involved. You can imagine their number as well as their interest. You need to enlist the support of your children as they are directly affected by your decision to remarry.

The Bible allows remarriage if one spouse dies, or if a spouse obtains a letter of 'divorcement' of Moses. Paul also says that if a spouse dies, the husband/wife is free to remarry. However, there is no reference to children. It goes without saying that each decision made is individualistic. Generally speaking, women find it difficult to remarry if they have children from their former relationship. This is understandable, considering the huge responsibility they shoulder. In addition, they can come against opposition from their in-laws, who may accuse them of unfaithfulness towards their dead son/brother. Some may even be accused of 'getting rid' of their husbands in order to remarry. In some cultures, such widows risk losing everything left behind by their late husbands, except the responsibility they have towards their children. A single mum should ask herself, "will I be capable of managing two homes put into one?" The choice is yours. So let the wisdom of God direct you with godly guidance.

CHAPTER 8
NAVIGATING THE IMPACT OF SINGLE PARENTING ON CHILDREN

Children born in two-parent homes feel the separation the most and they are the most vulnerable. If separation was an option for their parents, they shouldn't have gotten married at all, let alone have children. God would have 'thanked' them for it, for children are the 'heritage of God,' not of any man or woman.

Couples tend to forget their children during their periods of conflict. At times, the children may become weapons of war in the hands of parents, forgetting that, at every shot, ammunition does not only destroy the target but the weapon also. Be wise and keep in mind that you can endure the loss of all other things, but not your children. Once you have them in the right standing, you have not lost anything. So, be sure you keep them in focus at all times.

Weigh your actions in every situation, including reacting negatively on difficult occasions. The interest of children should be taken into consideration.

Please take time to read what Job says:

> *"Even a tree . . . If it is cut down, it will sprout again and grow new branches. Though its roots have grown old in the earth and its stump decays, at the scent of water it will bud and sprout again like a new seedling.*
>
> — JOB 14:7-9 NLT

That verse is instructive for single parents. It's almost like Job is pleading with single parents not to destroy their children, (who are the shoot) because they have lost the stump, (their homes.) Do not allow your children to become casualties of your war, for they are your destiny in which your seed is hidden. You may not be able to save your relationship, but you don't have to lose your children as well. They may, in most cases, be the only gain you have in the relationship. The fact is, while all other gains you may have are temporal, decaying and disappearing, however, by the mercy, forgiveness and the grace of God, your children are the preserves of God for all eternity.

The above could be frightening and could make some people rethink their decision. To others, whatever is out there cannot make them relent because there are marital conditions that are worse than divorce. There are women who gave their lives while saving their marriages. They should be highly commended, and the Lord Himself will care for and protect their children.

Visiting the home of their absent parent may be difficult at first but should become better as time goes on. If their feelings change after any visit, you need to know why. Let them tell you without forcing them to do so. If they don't want to talk about it but let the feelings evaporate soon after, fine. However, if the same repeats itself, you may have to ask them to let you know why. This is very important to their state of mind. If visiting could become another source of further damage, you may have to suspend it till they are more mature. There is no justification for the past to continue to impact negatively upon their overall well-being and their future.

Be free with your children so they are ready to confide in you; talk to them, and dialogue together. Allow them to bare their feelings to you.

Be ready to listen to them so they can let you know how the situation is affecting them. Don't keep important facts from them. They have the right to know what is happening to them before any other, as it will be highly embarrassing to them if they have to pick up facts about themselves from the public arena. However, please don't overload them with how you feel so as not to escalate their frustration.

You need to know how they are faring in school. Don't wait till their academic performance and moral behaviour are affected before you know. It might be too late to restore their God-given potential. You also need to keep a line of communication free between you and their teachers. To enable your children to become successful, make friends with them, because they are now your 'comrades in arms.' Please make efforts to attend events in their schools; as the only parent on ground, they can't afford your being absent from school events.

As soon as your matter gets to the public domain, the tempo will change dramatically for your children. They may become stereotyped by the majority of people and organisations around them as simply 'evil' because they come from 'broken homes.' They are treated and labelled offenders even before they start to behave. Some might even be accused of perpetrating disorders where they were not present. It is not uncommon to see married couples discouraging their children from relating with children of single parents. Some don't even allow such children to enter their homes.

At schools, their situation is pathetic. Some school authorities might not be doing enough for these innocent kids as they are not given enough care and support needed to withstand the storm in their lives. They are daily confronted with psychological and emotional challenges. If care is not taken, such children are likely to react negatively and might become unfriendly towards their mates as well as being at loggerheads with the school authorities. This evil has no end, as such children might be expelled from school eventually.

As a further reaction to their treatment, in developed countries, where there are social services, some of these children easily get into trouble with the state through law enforcement agents—the police. This is endless, as they may be involved with drugs, alcohol and prostitution. The majority of cases against such children are likely to land them in prison.

It is highly advisable for both parents to actively engage in caring for their children's well-being. Hence, leaving the responsibility solely to one parent to manage all the financial aspects is not a viable choice. This assertion couldn't be farther from reality. However, if certain circumstances arise that deviate from this norm, a thorough reassessment is warranted. Opting out or refusing to contribute to the upbringing of one's own children must be reconsidered, as such a decision could potentially inflict enduring adverse consequences on the children.

Younger children demand more care and attention than older ones. So if you find yourself having to cope with very young children alone, you need help. If your mother has the time, energy and love to help you stay at home while you run around for your needs, you are lucky. There are nurseries all around, but they cost so much money. Furthermore, getting a two- or one-year old early in the morning to get out of bed and to a nursery could be an upheaval. Both of you are better off having someone stay at home with the under-school age.

CHAPTER 9
YOU NEED HELP

SEEKING HELP FROM ABOVE

Single parents need help, and the most important is the help that comes from above. The psalmist says

"I look up to the mountains—does my help come from there? My help comes from the Lord, who made heaven and earth."

— PSALM 121:1-2 NLT

When Jesus was being taken into heaven, He promised us that He would send the Holy Spirit as our Helper, which He did. Surrender to Him, and He will take care of you. You need human help, and the Holy Spirit will direct you to the right people. He knows who will genuinely help you to cope with your present situation. Therefore you need to be filled and be led, empowered and dependent on His leading. He will enlighten you to pray according to the will of God for your life since He knows the mind of God concerning your present state.

Women, be the visionaries for your children. According to one writer,

> "A vision we give to others of who and what they could become, has power, when it echoes what the Spirit has already spoken into their souls."
>
> — LARRY CRABB

It follows, therefore, that the role of the Holy Spirit of God is very paramount in bringing up our children, as they need His power to achieve their dreams.

Teach and help them make the right choices in life. We shouldn't allow the pressure of caring for them to minimise what ought to be prioritised. How, then, can we keep our priorities in place? We do this by making prayer and the Word of God our top priority. Let Jesus walk ahead and alongside you every day because no one can raise children successfully without Him.

One other important way to set their lives moving in the right direction, through the help of the Holy Spirit, is to make them dream of a bright future for themselves, and this should start with you. What do you want them to become? Dream for them while they are still young with prayers and supplication to the One who holds their future. You need to surround yourself with the right people as well as your community. God Himself wants us to share our burdens with the right people, not those that will take advantage of our temporary peculiar situation. When Moses told God of the overwhelming weight of leading His people (the Israelites) to the Promised Land, God asked him to choose seventy men to help him.

We all have the privilege of asking for help from God, who will direct us to the right places. Pooling together all available resources around you—families, friends, communities, co-workers and the church of God—plus the blessing of the Holy Spirit will accomplish more than you ever think is possible.

The Bible, backed by the Holy Spirit, is the greatest helper. God's word is settled in heaven, and no demon can unsettle it (Psalm 119:89). As a respected Welsh preacher once said,

> "It is the Spirit and the word, the Spirit upon the word and the Spirit in us as we read the word."
>
> — MARTYN LLOYD-JONES

The word without the Spirit is dead, "for letter killeth, but the spirit giveth life" (2 Corinthians 3:6b). When we overwhelm ourselves with issues outside our control, we cripple the Spirit to work on our behalf, and when the word is made impotent, we say God is far away. However, the assurance of the word of God is made manifest throughout the Scriptures. As Jesus Christ is the same yesterday, today and forever, so also the word of God in print. As long as it is called 'today' with the sun shining in the sky, God's word remains unchangeable, unrelenting and immutable.

Its application with faith results in victory. Jesus assured us that with God, we can do all things, and when asked in faith, nothing is impossible (Luke 18:27). Therefore, when we are overwhelmed by our situation, let us remember to go back to the Scriptures. One preacher said, when we are confused, let God be the first to call upon for help. In the Scriptures, we have all the answers we need at every stage of life. In fact, the Bible is the only Book that has given answers to every question the world will ever ask. As the greatest Book ever read, copies are available everywhere, even at places where copies have been forbidden!

The Word of God, which is Spirit and Power, has the capacity to penetrate through any barrier without breaking any physical structure. The angel of God led Apostle Peter out of prison by the Word without opening the iron gates with all the sentries on guard. As Apostle Paul said, even though he was in chains, the word of God could not be put in chains. In effect, we have access to it if and when we desire. As a single parent, your best companion and friend is the Bible. In it, there is no deceit, no condemnation and no justification for unrepentant sinners. Conversely, in it, we have forgiveness of sin, love, justification through the blood of the Lamb and eternal life. It goes without saying, therefore, that whatever you need to cope with the huge responsibility thrust on you is readily accessible.

Let us look at some of the potential questions single parents are bound to ask and the readily available answers found in the Bible. As a single parent, many people will distance themselves from you, as you are seen as a type of plague that can contaminate others. You, therefore, conclude that no one loves you. In Jeremiah 31:3, God says that He has loved you with an everlasting love—a love that lasts forever! Only God has that capacity, so the love of others becomes secondary. Please pay attention to the phrase *"He has loved you"*, just like *"while we were yet sinners, Jesus died for us."* Both phrases indicate that God's provision has been in place before our need arises. What a Wonder!

The story of the woman at the well with Jesus is an amazing example of God loving us "while we were yet sinners." If God could love us in our fallen state, how much more love will He shower on us when we come to Him in repentance? Again when you feel like 'throwing in the towel' as a result of too much to do, God says in 2 Corinthians 12:9 that His grace that helps us do extraordinary things is made available to us in its sufficiency. Do you know there is no "can't do" in your compass, the Bible? Yet it is a daily song of many, even among the children of God. If our Father in Heaven says He can do all things, it is also expected that His children should take after Him. After all, God said He made Moses a god unto Pharaoh, Exodus 7:1 and we are called gods in Psalms 82:6. 'God' here simply means someone in command or in control of their environment or situation. God is the Divine Controller of His creation and has given us everything that pertains to godliness and righteousness with which each of us should be in dominion. We are therefore enabled to do all things in Christ who strengthens us. So it is not you doing anything but the strength of Christ in you.

In Ephesians 2:10, the Bible says:

> *"For we are His workmanship, created in Christ Jesus unto good works, which God hath before ordained that we should walk in them."*
>
> — EPHESIANS 2:10 KJV

Therefore what we are doing now has already been pre-programmed into our lives. It is not us doing anything spectacular, but God is working His good works through all those who are willing to yield themselves unto Him. So see every task as being doable as the Bible says,

> *"I can do all things through Christ who strengthens me."*
>
> — PHILIPPIANS 4:13 NKJV

This realisation will make your days anxiety-free, knowing full well that you are not in charge.

EMBRACING COMMUNITY AND CHURCH SUPPORT

For Christians and others, the Church is one of the most useful institutions that cater for the physical, emotional, psychological and spiritual well-being of those who are hurting and needing help. I say "Christians and others" because the Church of God is wide open to whoever will come—Christians and non-Christians alike. In an article titled "Where Sinners Go" written by David Branon in *Our Daily Bread* of 8 January 2013, a Christian asked his non-Christian friend "Bob, do you know where sinners go?" He was quick to reply, "That's easy." "You're going to tell me they go to hell." However, to Bob's surprise, his friend informed him that they go to church, as it is the hospital for sinners and not a club of saints. In some big Churches, there are counselling sessions in addition to prayers; and their work and help are free. This is God's work, and their reward is from Him. Don't hesitate to seek help.

Psalms 68:6 says that God places the lonely in families—families of believers (i.e. the Church). If the Church is only concerned with those who are whole, well, complete and righteous, then its work is half done. Jesus says He has not come to call the just and the whole but for the fallen, the lonely and the sick to repentance in order to bring them back to Himself. If the emphasis is only on the flawless, the Church is not helping Christ in His mission.

Failure may be an option but never the only option. What we call failure is not *falling down* but *staying down*. Single parents may be in a fallen state, but not a failure, if they refuse to remain on the ground. They need help, encouragement and assurance that they can start all over again and have a good life.

Naomi, Ruth and Orpah found themselves in an unusual fellowship which transcended age, race, culture and status. They had something in common; the death of their husbands created a bond between them, and so were able to comfort each other. Therefore when seeking help, you will gain more from those who have walked the same path you are now walking. The Bible says that God is beautiful in all situations. His Spirit, as Comforter, is the only One who lessens pain and lets you see whatever good there is in the seemingly ugly situation, just as Ruth did and was heavenly rewarded.

COPING WITH STRESS AND EXPLORING AVAILABLE SOURCES OF HELP

As much as you take advice from others in your shoes, remember your situation is not the same as theirs. To avoid stress, don't be pressured into meeting their standards overnight. Go at your own pace in line with your needs, especially as it affects your children.

As you manage to get through each day, always remember that the enemy has not taken over the steering wheel of your life from God. He (God) is firmly in control of everything, whether we know it or not. His plan for your life is still intact. As long as life lasts, you can still achieve your dreams.

There are numerous help tips on the internet free of charge, too. As always, just like television, the internet contains "the good, the bad and the ugly." You, therefore, need a discerning spirit to access materials that will influence your life positively.

As their parent and the only adult in the house, you need to seek help from trusted relations and friends as well as professionals in matters concerning your children and family. In the end, it is you who will coordinate and finalise what suits your own condition. You are in charge and, therefore, responsible and accountable for every decision taken.

In the past, communities contributed immensely to children's upbringing. Elders would correct any child misbehaving outside their home. All that is now lost as communities have virtually disappeared as a result of industrialisation/globalisation. There is no more trust between neighbours, even if you know them closely. Nearly everyone is suspicious of the other person. All these go to create societies alienated from each other. However, there are varieties of affordable childcare centres. The important thing is that they should be of good quality. There are friendly staff who pay close attention to young children. In childcare centres, children learn to be independent while away from home, more tolerant of their peers and friendly towards each other. Relations are still at hand to help in some cultures till now. That, again, is being fragmented as a result of young couples moving away from home.

In the developed world, a lot of childcare centres exist whose costs are subsidised by either federal or local governments. This is primarily to encourage lone parents to work. You need not keep your young children at home longer than necessary because they may find it difficult to socialise or integrate with their peers when they are of school age. Most church organisations have Sunday school sessions for children on Sundays and some evenings during weekdays. These are very educative. Children start to make friends with others at an early age. With all these, you start to enjoy a bit of freedom and even find time to attend to some other pressing needs. By and large, if you, as a single parent, want to work, you need to do a sort of research into what help you can get. There are various types of financial help for lone parents of young children of preschool age. You can get help if you wish to go back to school or college.

In the Western World, there are organisations fully committed to helping single parents. Some governments render financial help, too, which has been discussed earlier. The fact is you will need help at some point or the other on your journey as a single parent. When, where and how you need the help will depend on individual disposition. Some may brace up and launch themselves headlong to show their determination to succeed, while others may remain shocked and confused and just go through the motions in the early part of single parenting. In either case, when the need arises to seek help, don't hesitate to ask.

GETTING HELP FROM RELATIONS AND FRIENDS

Having so much to cope with could be demoralising and stressful, and if care is not taken, can affect your performance at work. Stress is one of the negative symptoms of being a single parent and, if not well managed, could develop into illness. So be honest with yourself and seek help. Don't forget, if you push yourself beyond the limit and breakdown or are hospitalised, someone or others will step into your shoes, which could be very painful and fearful for your children. The idea of having none of their parents with them could be devastating. So please ask for help in time to avoid any major calamity. You should remember, everyone knows that you are doing the work of two people. Not everyone will say: 'serves you right' or that 'you ask for it'. There are those who will not judge you but help you. So go for such people to stay afloat. If you refuse to ask for help, your condition may deteriorate. Take time to relax and rest. Yes! You need to, and you will discover how refreshing it can be.

Evidence abounds that stress could lead to depression. Depression makes one touchy and temperamental. When that happens, people will begin to avoid you, and you may be given labels that do not actually explain your true condition. This is neither good for you nor your children. It is a real distraction and a cog in your wheel of progress.

Sleep is a very good medicine. You gain a lot of energy back through sound sleep. The whole man is rested – body, soul and spirit. Make sure you get the necessary hours of sleep everyday, where and when possible. If your children are still young, this may be a tall order, as your sleeping hours are dependent on when they sleep. Yet bear it in mind that sleeping well keeps you all going, as a consistent lack of it for a long period of time is bound to affect your health and well-being.

If you are awake in the night and find it difficult to go back to sleep, seize the opportunity to sing songs of praise, and you will find rest. Please avoid crowding your mind with unresolved issues, which only lead to sleeplessness and tiredness.

As discussed earlier, asking for help is not a show of weakness, so explore what help is available from your relations and friends. Now that your own relations are nearer to you than before, you need to encourage your children to make friends with their cousins. That is not to say that you should discard your ex's relations if they are willing to relate with your family. You might be surprised to know that quite a number remain your silent sympathisers for obvious reasons. When they run into your children where they need not look over their shoulders, such people will go all out to care for them. However, you need to be careful as such relationships may not augur well with those who are not your friends in the family. Those 'friends' might be branded traitors. This is just a caution.

Don't hesitate to stop those not contributing positively to your well-being. You have enough to deal with, and there is no need for anyone to pollute your children's innocent minds. The most important fact about relations and friends is to be friendly with them, not acting suspiciously towards them and at the same time, getting a grip on your situation so you cease from becoming their regular topic for discussion. A constant reminder of what has happened to you will only set you back. What you need right now is those who will move you forward rather than those who are only interested in the past you are trying to forget. Such discussions are damaging and could be very offensive to you and especially to your children, who may not particularly welcome any adverse comment about their absentee parent.

SEEKING PROFESSIONAL HELP

There are, however, professionals whose role is very objective. They have no side to take in your matter. It may seem embarrassing at first to talk to complete strangers. You should take solace in the fact that your case does not go beyond the four walls of their office, as it is unethical, and any leakage of your discussion is likely to earn the organisation litigation. In addition, the majority of them may not recognise you in the shopping mall. Their work is almost as private as seeing your doctor. So you can confide in them rather than friends and relations. Their professional expertise and experience have given them an edge over laypeople. However, in order to have a balanced assessment of any issue, it is advisable to keep both sides active.

CHAPTER 10
APPROACHES TO DISCIPLINE IN SINGLE PARENTING

DISCIPLINE AS A FOUNDATION FOR EFFECTIVE PARENTING

It is imperative that you will deal with actions and reactions, starting with your own, before you help your children to deal with theirs. Overreacting escalates tension. It is advisable to always act rather than react. Discipline is not necessarily punishment but 'to teach' as the Bible says:

> *"Train up a child in the way he should go: and when he is old, he will not depart from it."*
>
> — PROVERBS 22:6 KJV

However, **training involves discipline.** Without discipline during training sessions, it will be difficult both for the trainer and the trainee to achieve their goal.

> As a single parent, when you punish a child for being upset about the situation you brought on them, you aren't fair to them. Don't forget, if you become too harsh with them, they are left with no one to turn to and this could have a devastating effect on them or drive them out of the house. Children usually act out their emotions because they find it difficult to talk or express how they feel to adults without offending or causing more trouble. Their emotions could be played out in many different ways. Some can start to steal, wet their beds and tell lies, while others may become moody and confused. Their school performance may be affected and in some cases, this could lead to some more serious outcomes, like taking drugs, becoming violent, etc.

Find out what lies beneath their bad behaviour and deal with it. Reiterate your commitment to their well-being by dialoguing with them as often as possible. Encourage them to make friends, and visit your relations, especially those with children of their age bracket.

Having family meetings is a very good way of letting each one have a say in how the home is run. After all, they are now your *comrade-in-arms*. Everyone should have a say, even the youngest, so whatever you agree upon will be honoured by all. Yours should not be an autocratic regime, but rather more of a democracy, with you still holding the reins of affairs.

Apart from making decisions, getting together on a regular basis reinforces togetherness, love and understanding. Family meetings enable each one to share personal aspirations with others. The older ones, with their wealth of experience, have the advantage of advising the younger ones on the right way to go. Children of all ages have the privilege of accessing information from each other more than adults simply because they speak out their minds freely without fear or favour. Consequently, friends of children of single parents might pass on to them, unknowingly, what their parents have discussed about the single-parent home. Such information, when received with a clear mind, might be useful in any way to moving the family forward.

Now that you are responsible for your children in almost everything, you need to be sure and firm in dealing with them. The Bible asks in Hebrews 12:7,

> *". . . Who ever heard of a child who is never disciplined by its father?"*
>
> — HEBREWS 12:7 NLT

Discipline in every area of life is an important key to successful living. The Bible says that discipline is not sweet at the time of its application, however, if well received, more often than not, results in balanced and responsible adults. However uncaring a parent may be, it is doubtful if anyone wants their children to be at odds with the law, if only for the sake of their own name that could be dragged in the mud.

Nevertheless, children do get into trouble partly as a result of a lack of discipline or inadequate enforcement of correction. High Priest Eli only stated the truth but never enforced it. If children have passed the physical 'rod', use the spiritual 'rod' on them. Eli would not have incurred the wrath of God if he had stripped his children of their priesthood and all the privileges attached to the office. By doing so, Israel would not have been defeated by their enemies.

In training up your children as a single parent, you may tend to be hard on them, an action that does no one any good. Admittedly, when children of single parents offend, society is quick to blame their parents as a result of the condition they find themselves in. When children of couples and singles offend, a greater punishment is put on the single-parent child, while the children of couples may go unpunished. At times, the child of a single parent might be accused of influencing the couple's children. The above, notwithstanding, is no excuse for you to be too hard on your kids, otherwise you might drive them out of the house to a society that has nothing to offer them. Do your part to show them the way and, at the same time, walk on the same path yourself. Once you do your part, God is committed to doing His own.

Single parents, in order not to be judged as a failure, tend to over-stretch their children's capabilities. By striving to make them flawless, you might be working against their God-given potential. Do not encourage your children to be what they are not cut out to be, because they will not fit in. Rather, work to convince them that they are of much value to God because of who they are and much more when they fulfil their God-given goals.

Praise their efforts, whether successful or otherwise, and let them see mistakes as opportunities to learn how to make wrong right.

DON'T BE BITTER

What has happened to you is part of life, otherwise, it would not have existed. Betrayal is no stranger to our world. Judas betrayed Jesus, and Peter denied Him also, yet He offered both of them a pathway to salvation. Judas declined the way to life and committed suicide, believing that forgiveness was beyond him, whereas the scriptures make us understand that while we were yet sinners Christ died for us. In other words, Judas' sin is included in the sins for which Jesus died. On the other hand, Peter repented of his own sin and was forgiven and was mightily used by Jesus to establish His Church. If Jesus could forgive Peter and us, showing us an example to follow, we too ought to and must forgive others who might have wronged us. Jesus was deeply hurt by what Judas and Peter did, so it is impossible for us to go through life too without being hurt.

Jesus was never bitter against Peter and Judas and us also because He knew that everything works for good for all those who put their trust in God.

Joseph, an ordinary human being like us, was deeply hurt by what his brothers did to him, selling him off from their midst. In the process, he became a slave, but God was with him. As if being a slave was not enough, he was lied against and, without trial, was thrown into prison. Yet in all these, he remained joyful. There was no record of him avenging the evil done to him by his brothers, and he never asked for judgement upon them either. Rather than seizing the opportunity thrust at him to take revenge when his brothers came to Egypt to buy food from him, he told them what only a few would say:

> *". . . And he said, I am Joseph your brother, whom you sold into Egypt! But now, do not be distressed and disheartened or vexed and angry with yourselves because you sold me here, for God sent me ahead of you to preserve life.*
>
> *God sent me before you to preserve for you a posterity and to continue a remnant on the earth, to save your lives by a great escape and save for you many survivors.*
>
> *So now it was not you who sent me here, but God: and He has made me a father to Pharaoh and lord of all his house and ruler over all the land of Egypt."*

— GENESIS 45:4-5, 7-8 AMPC

Joseph must have seen beyond all his troubles and concentrated on his future. He excelled in everything he did, including being head of servants and slaves as well as being the head of prisoners. Excellency was, therefore, not new to him when he became the Prime Minister of Egypt.

You should, therefore, see beyond your present calamity and start to picture the end you desire. Jesus saw beyond Peter's betrayal and fallen state as well as beyond our own sinfulness, knowing full well that if we trust Him and forgive others as He has forgiven us, nothing can keep us from becoming what God has ordained us to become. Don't let your feelings run wild, or else you may lose your balance. Take one step at a time. At times, you may be frightened and overwhelmed by the huge task before you. It is expected, so don't deny how you feel or suppress your emotions. Denial can be damaging to your overall well-being.

Learn to eliminate all bitterness from your thoughts and communication. Stop pulling yourself and your children back to your old life that you fled from and which you are to forget. Bitterness is likened to a seed that can germinate and grow to produce fruits. It should not be allowed to live, so uproot, kill and burn it. Stop remembering the details of your past except if you want to use it for others to learn from it. How can God fill us with good things when we allow ourselves to be home for bitterness and all forms of evil thoughts? Therefore forgetting the past is not optional, it is 'the deal' if you want to succeed. God says through prophet Isaiah:

> *"Remember ye not the former things, neither consider the things of old. Behold, I will do a new thing, now it shall spring forth; shall ye not know it? I will even make a way in the wilderness, and rivers in the desert."*
>
> — ISAIAH 43:18-19 KJV

God is saying that as long as we cleave to the past, the future and all its blessings will not become a reality. As God always means what He says and says only what He means, there is no forgiveness for the unforgiving.

MANAGING ANGER

> *"Be angry, and do not sin: do not let the sun go down on your wrath"*
>
> — EPHESIANS 4:26 NKJV

This is at variance with human anger that lasts decades or even to the grave. However, if you embrace this godly principle, you will soon be living your life devoid of anger and tension. Anger is an evil spirit and very destructive. James says that our anger can't serve any useful purpose, and it does not work the righteousness of God (James 1:20).

If the Bible says we can be angry but not sin, it means there has to be an expression of anger but in a safe manner. Anger can't be kept forever, it will come up sooner or later, and the longer it is kept, the more destructive and violent it can be. So, with the help of the Holy Spirit, your anger will not dominate you by growing into an uncontrollable monster. One good and helpful way to express anger or feeling is writing it down. A long time ago, the children of an elderly woman made her very angry. She decided to put her anger on paper. Pages upon pages, she told the story of her ordeal. Amazingly, she discovered that it brought her a sense of forgiveness towards her children. However, she kept the document for a while, and it started to remind her about the ordeal she went through until she decided to inform her aged father. After reading it to him, the old man asked how she felt. She said she was relieved. Her father prayed for her and asked that the document be burnt there and then. That burning brought an end to the anger forever.

CULTIVATING ACTIVE LISTENING

Listening attentively is a skill to be learnt, as it is very effective. It shows you value the person and what they have to say. When you listen, you are likely to grasp the concept of the situation, what to do about it and how to get it done.

THE DANGER OF LABELS

Labelling is counter-productive. You need to know what your children or you yourself have done to earn such labelling. In addition, labelling does not disclose the reason for the label and is not likely going to result in any meaningful change. So don't label your child or allow any other person to do so, be it in school or in your neighbourhood. Don't forget to employ friendly means to correct situations you are not in agreement with. What we say and how we say it can either make or mar a relationship. Therefore you can label what a child has done, which is subject to change, but not the child.

CHAPTER II
EMBRACING CHANGE

The godly change we need can only come by prayers. The real change we need is divine and since it is spiritual, it is only possible through divine intervention. Paul says,

> *"But we all ... are being transformed ... by the Spirit of the Lord."*
>
> — 2 CORINTHIANS 3:18 NIV

Any attempt to effect change through carnal means is likely to be resisted by the one that has power over the flesh – Satan. Prayer is the greatest agent of change and as we engage in fervent prayers for ourselves and our children, God is committed to making the necessary changes in our lives. For a lasting change, it has to come from inside and as said earlier, only the Spirit of God can effect that kind of change.

Change is the most important thing that has happened to you in your situation. Most of us resist change including the major change of losing a relationship. However, when this inevitable happens, it is followed by a series of other changes, which normally result from the loss of your relationship. The loss and the change it brings can help to develop your character. Just because you are lost between the past you know and the future you don't know is no cause to become overwhelmed because what once was is now no more. Be assured that even on the dark road, God said He is with you. In Isaiah 42:16, God promised

> *". . . I will lead them in paths they have not known. I will make darkness light before them, and crooked places straight. These things I will do for them, and not forsake them."*
>
> — ISAIAH 42:16 NKJV

Be courageous enough to change yourself to improve your circumstances. Don't be surprised to learn that a relationship fails as a result of the negative contribution of the people involved and the misunderstanding that brings it to its bitter end—yours inclusive! When you change your outlook, your mind and attitude, you discover that certain things will automatically change, as a change from old ways of doing things leads to different and acceptable results.

The change process has a price attached to it and must not be avoided, or else the price of never improving will be paid. The price of endurance is essential when passing through the difficulties of change if we are not to end up with a worse kind of pain. So don't just change enough to get away from your former troubles, let your change be strong and healthy enough to solve your problems.

Changing your name is a departure from the past if you wish. Adult children may frown at changing your name, which might be a sign of breaking the last link they have with their other parent. There might be reactions and counter-reactions to name change. Your ex's relations who would otherwise have maintained a close connection with their children would feel dishonoured by your name change. However, only what will contribute positively to a child's well-being should be considered paramount in any given situation both now and in the future. Losing a name is a loss of identity and not every child will like it. So discuss with them, if they are old enough, before any name change.

VICTORY OVER THE FLESH: GATEWAY TO MEANINGFUL CHANGE

We care much more for our physical appearance than we do our inward man. However, how we look to God is more important than how others see us. The Bible says God looks on the inside but men look at the outside. The inside is the real man, while the outside could be a façade. In order to put off the old and put on the new, Chuck Swindoll, quoted in *Word for Today* Saturday 20 December 2008, says:

> The number one enemy of change is the hard-core, self-sustained sin nature within you. Like a spoilt child, it's been gratified and indulged for years, so it won't give up without a temper tantrum. The flesh dies a slow, bitter, bloody death; kicking and struggling all the way. Lasting change takes place in first gear, not overdrive. So expect occasional setbacks, and don't let them derail you. When you feel like throwing in the towel, get down on your knees and ask God to help you get back on track. He'll do it.

CHAPTER 12

RELATIONSHIP WITH THE CHILDREN IN THIS DIGITAL AGE

SAFEGUARDING YOUR CHILDREN'S EXPOSURE

One very crucial task for single mothers is to monitor what their children watch on television, on the internet and on social media, as this age could truly be described as an age of great confusion. It is an age of too much knowledge – knowing how to operate TVs and Internet but hardly knowing why they should be so engrossed with them. Children cannot fully comprehend what adverse effect these information technologies could have on them.

PARENTAL RESPONSIBILITY IN MANAGING THE INFLUENCE OF MEDIA ON YOUNG MINDS

The Bible says we are what we read, watch, hear and take in. Horror films breed violent adults and watching sexual acts on TV will result in sexual perversion. The Internet is a gateway to all sorts of both good and evil practices. While the TV entertains and educates us, our relationship with it is usually one-sided. Even if we are to respond to it, it takes time to do so and there are those moderating what goes out into the public. This is not so with the Internet. It is personal, private and dangerous for both adults and children, especially children. There have been a series of cases over the years of children who have been lured into danger or even death by those they met on the Internet.

If therefore people are made up of what they take into their heart, parents have responsibilities to help them guard their hearts. In Proverbs 4:23, the Bible says:

> *"keep thy heart with all diligence; for out of it are the issues of life."*
>
> — PROVERBS 4:23 KJV

The heart is the centre of the whole man. Whatever captures the heart captures the man. Whatever comes out of the heart of any man is a sure representative of the man. So we need to help our children guard their hearts/minds against all forms of evil flying all around with the help of the Holy Spirit. Once the heart is defiled, the whole man is defiled also.

Jesus says that out of what has been built into our inner mind, our mouths will speak. It therefore, follows that children will be what you help them make of themselves. You are the overseer, or as the Bible put it, the bishop of both your heart and their own.

Apart from safeguarding your children spiritually, as well as from the negative influence of television, the internet, paedophiles and peer groups, their total well-being is of utmost importance. You must be very friendly with their teachers to keep lines of communication always open. This enables you to discuss any issue with them without tension or faultfinding. This calls for being sensitive to their needs to the point of sacrificing everything you have for their wellbeing.

Think about your children as a mixed bag of strengths and weaknesses, virtues and vices. If you are looking for perfection in your relationship with them, you have missed it. Your only path to a successful relationship with them is to love and accept them as they are. The myth that others are 'normal' out there except those in your life is a farce. If that is your school of thought, you will spend the rest of your life fixing and controlling them, while they, on the other hand, will live under an illusion that they are something they are not. If you love your children as you profess to be, you will focus on their strengths and support them in areas of struggle.

TAKING BETTER DECISIONS

Whether you like it or not, past decisions brought you to where you are today. It is therefore imperative that if you desire better outcomes in the future, learn to make better decisions today. As you are not making decisions for yourself alone, involve the other key players as well, while you seek the counsel of well-meaning people. At the forefront of the decision-making process are some basic principles. Do not be drawn into making decisions with long-lasting effects during your temporary situation. Such decisions are likely to be the product of your present emotions and quickly become obsolete as soon as you regain yourself. Take one step at a time and try not to do so many things at the same time. Prioritise matters and don't fight on all fronts at the same time. Because you have so much to do, 24 hours may not be enough in a day for you, so there is no room for time wastage. Within all these, you still need to build in time for rest and real relaxation so as not to crash!

MIND WHAT YOU SAY

In your moments of anger and frustration, be careful what you say to your children and yourself. It is easy to vent our anger on the person we can see rather than those not around. However, what we say about ourselves impacts more on us than what others say to us. God told the Israelites in Numbers 14:28 that as they said in His ears He would do to them. The people said they were going to die in the wilderness along with their children, but God answered, *"No! Only you would die and not your children because I am taking your children to the Promised Land as I promised to your forefathers."* Therefore, none of what others say to you counts, as God, first and most important, and you second, have the final say over your life and that of your children. Let us enter into God's covenant of good and not of evil and start to say what He says about us.

CHAPTER 13
YOUR FUTURE RELATIONSHIP WITH YOUR EXES

A broken relationship with children who are also deeply hurt within it serves as a tangible illustration of a connection that is vividly alive and significantly dynamic. It is, however, everything but peace and harmony. Whoever you are, you are not capable of manning the whole situation. After all, you are just a mother or father and can never be both. In essence, there is an emptiness somewhere in the hearts of your children, which the person on ground cannot fill.

An end to your marriage relationship marks the beginning of a new relationship with your children, your ex-wife/husband and their relatives, your own family, and friends, some of whom might not see your point of view and therefore appear to be on your ex's side. In addition to these relations are the people in the new marriage relationship made by your ex-spouse. This is a relationship that is often used to bring the first one to an abrupt end. If it had not existed, maybe there might not have been any suggestion of bringing the existing one to an end. As Adam had no one around to replace Eve, their union continued. These are all relationships you have to cope with. How then, do you handle them without worsening an already sore situation?

Bob Gas, Author of Word for Today gave a very powerful advice thus:

> ## "DON'T BEGIN UNTIL YOU COUNT THE COST"
>
> A counsellor who had a friend contemplating divorce writes: She didn't want to hear anything from us... she'd made up her mind. So in frustration, my friends and I compiled a list of what we wish we'd known before we got divorced. We'd each experienced the upheaval of divorce and watched our friends' second marriages end:
>
> **1. Life will change more than you realise:** Dividing assets isn't always equitable. Instead of two people parenting your children, if you have custody, you become the breadwinner,

spiritual advisor and disciplinarian. Stress levels become staggering. You ache to watch your children doling out their time in an effort not to alienate either parent. And the hassles don't end when your children grow up and marry, they continue with your grandchildren.

The above paragraph is true of every broken relationship. In some cultures, there might not be assets to divide. The woman is usually treated as if she did not contribute to the home for the time she was there and therefore leaves with nothing, except her children. In some cases, the man can even take the children from her. The woman will have to start from scratch. If she has had enough children at this juncture, she would have to live with her condition until her children are old enough to be able to relate with her without taking permission from their father.

In relation to the children, I believe they are the only ones that can give an account of what they went through or are still going through. They suffer unfairly as if they had a hand in their parents' conflicts. Parents even vex their frustration and anger on them. They are caught up in the web of years of struggle, malice and hatred from which some of them may not recover. Some of them become rebellious even when their parents put some ideas to them that could move them forward. It takes the grace and favour of God to restore them. As much as some children try to be part of their family, it is discovered that they are subtly being alienated by those now in control. No wonder, they quickly lose touch to the extent that grandchildren on both sides are not known to each other. Parents are usually responsible for erecting this 'firewall' between the two sides, probably in an attempt to deny that outside vital information about the family.

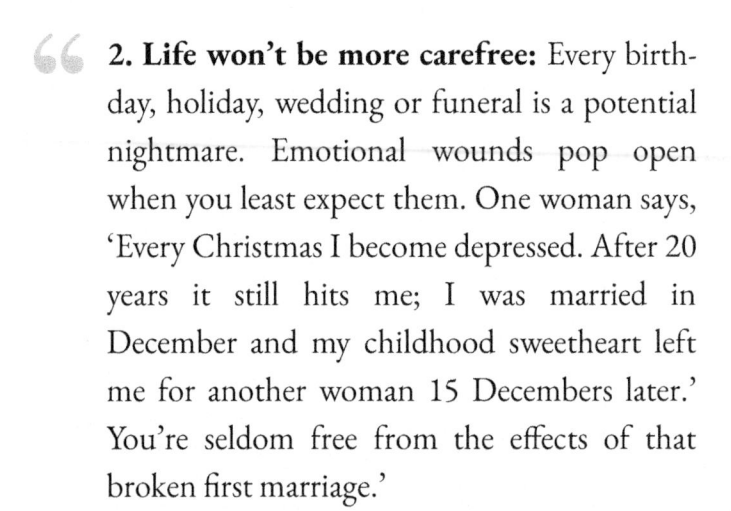

> **2. Life won't be more carefree:** Every birthday, holiday, wedding or funeral is a potential nightmare. Emotional wounds pop open when you least expect them. One woman says, 'Every Christmas I become depressed. After 20 years it still hits me; I was married in December and my childhood sweetheart left me for another woman 15 Decembers later.' You're seldom free from the effects of that broken first marriage.'

In order to save yourself from old wounds popping up at family gatherings, you can reduce your attendance to the important ones. However, there is no way by which you can excuse yourself from your children's marriages, especially girls whose marriage ceremonies are expected to be held in their father's house, though they have no relationship with the home. However, these are the occasions when members of the two families meet each other after several years of separation. In many cases, these families may not even know their child that is getting married! There is an artificial atmosphere here, for the one reason that the children involved do not belong. Nevertheless, the mother or her relations should make the day glorious for the sake of their daughter with the consolation that the ceremony of artificiality will soon be over to pave the way for reality. Care must be taken to avoid any tension developing.

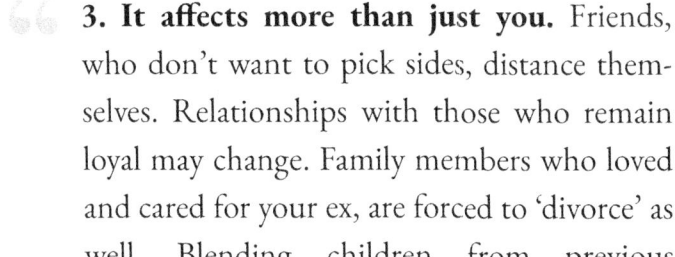

> **3. It affects more than just you.** Friends, who don't want to pick sides, distance themselves. Relationships with those who remain loyal may change. Family members who loved and cared for your ex, are forced to 'divorce' as well. Blending children from previous marriages brings problems...Life's more complicated than ever. Like children, we let our desire for momentary pleasure pull us from God's best, rather than doing the hard work it takes to turn short-term pain into long-term gain.

The above paragraph is the trickiest of them all. The question is, why should people take sides and what is its benefit? The interesting aspect of people's contribution to a broken relationship is hearing just one side of the story—no verification from the other side—and judgement is passed. From then on, they help to spread rumours, ideas and points of view of that one side, which are not likely to be totally true. Even after hearing both sides, do you know that you are not likely to be in possession of enough facts to give judgement? This is so for the single reason that whatever has transpired between the couple to trigger off a separation or divorce might never be uttered forever! God said the heart of man is desperately wicked, who can know it? (Jeremiah 17:9). Only God sees into the deepest mind and the wickedness it contains. Therefore, rather than taking sides, why not seek the good of the children by the advice you give to both sides and let them sort themselves out since they are adults? As the years roll by, most wounds are healed especially with people who know God. What becomes of those loyalists? However fragmented a family becomes, against all odds, the members are still related. It is not deniable and cannot be destroyed.

There is another evil to these 'intruders'. Some of them act as 'secret agents'. They can even befriend you in an attempt to have information about you, which they divulge to the other side. You may never know them, but they would have caused you considerable damage. There are some family members who wouldn't want to sever their relationship with either side. They are, however, agents too. They come under suspicion that they could be used to cause havoc.

Keeping in touch with the other parent and their relations is crucial but entails hard work because of the emotional circumstances surrounding such meetings. Such meetings might not go well at first, but this should not be a reason to stop them.

However, if your children are not enjoying it, which might stem from their relations' behaviour towards them—criticising you in their presence and the like—you might have to discuss with these relations, if you have any relationship with them, as a great percentage of such relations might choose to distance themselves or even become enemies. If there is no change to the situation, you may have to stop such arrangements as they can potentially destabilise your children. Their well-being should be of priority. Attending family events, festivals, birthdays and so on, may be traumatic for children living outside the family home, especially the younger ones.

CHAPTER 14
THE COMPLEXITY OF SECOND MARRIAGES

You need plenty of time to decide how to go about a new relationship especially if you have children whose ages will be a determining factor. If they are very young and need a lot of your time, you need wisdom to decide to take on an additional role as a new wife or partner. If the other partner has children too, blending both together requires a lot of hard work. If, on the other hand, your children are grown up, this is another cup of tea. You need to involve them at every stage of your new relationship if you don't want to collide forcefully with them. They have had enough trouble to this point in their lives and wouldn't want any add-ons. You may think they are selfish and too self-centred, but they might actually be saving you from calamities that may ensue in the future. So listen to them because, right now, they are more important to you than any new relationship you are yet to experience. If you are patient with them and with yourself, the right time is bound to come, so wait patiently. Don't forget that even when they grow up, they will continue to need you. If you are involved in another relationship, your relationship with your older family may become secondary and this may not augur well with them. So, think hard before you upset your current situation. Your children are entitled to be settled.

The issue of blending children from different sources might be very complicated and problematic. Think about it; if children from the same father and mother (who share some character traits) can find it difficult to live together in peace, what chances are there then for those from 'his' and 'her' former families?

BLENDING TWO FAMILIES

Single parents contemplating re-marriage have really hard work to do in resolving the problems that might accompany such moves, particularly in relation to children from both sides. First, every child is unique in their own right. It is, however, easier to blend younger children than teenage children and adults, as the latter already established their own way of doing things. Your authority is unlikely to carry weight with your older children as with the younger ones. Therefore you need to approach them with wisdom, understanding and patience, while your younger ones need nurture and security. Always remember that you have been calling the shots at every stage and you are now on your third level, which is more complicated than the ones that have gone before. Despite their non-involvement, each stage imparts differently on them. As they didn't ask to be pushed around different conditions, you need to be understanding and help strengthen their sense of security during periods of transition. Please always keep in focus the challenges involved in blending two families. There is no quick fix and do not expect instant acceptance or total compatibility.

Your condition becomes more complex by the time of your second marriage, especially when you have children involved. If because of your second marriage, your ex-spouse decides to take into custody his/her children, you may experience a personal sense of loss. If, afterwards, you do not have any child in your second relationship your situation may be worse off. Overlooking or refusing to acknowledge the complexity involved in the steps you are taking may result in frustration and anger. The approval of your adult children is very important if you want to avoid steep opposition and unrest that could follow. The truth is that children don't buy into such arrangements, which may appear selfish and unreasonable now. However, if you are able to 'bulldoze' your way through, the truth may become apparent in a few years' time, when it might be too late to put back the hand of the clock.

For those who want to remain committed to biblical values and cherish a good Christian conscience, Matthew 5:31 becomes a compass.

> *"It hath been said, Whosoever shall put away his wife, let him give her a writing of divorcement: But I say unto you, That whosoever shall put away his wife, saving for the cause of fornication, causeth her to commit adultery: and whosoever shall marry her that is divorced committeth adultery."*
>
> — MATTHEW 5:31 KJV

In such cases, much grace is required to remain single and whoever receives this grace will be glad for such a decision as years go by. One would have spared his or herself and the children more complications and the resultant troubles.

PART THREE
RESTORATION AND HEALING

CHAPTER 15
ON YOUR WAY TO RECOVERY

You need to recover from your loss, and there are keys to this recovery. Let us consider some of them in this chapter.

RECOVERY STARTS WITH ACKNOWLEDGING YOUR FEELINGS

When you are aggrieved, the normal thing is to be angry, fearful, depressed, resentful and helpless. There is no denying their existence because God created us with feelings and will not expect us to be happy when we are grieving. Take everything to Him in prayers, pour out your heart and according to His word, He will comfort you.

SEEKING SUPPORT AND OVERCOMING ISOLATION

Care must be taken not to isolate yourself by shutting your door on everyone, thinking that they are all against you. You need the support and encouragement of people around you provided you don't make enemies out of them. Paul, the Apostle of Jesus Christ, admonishes us from the Bible to help each other to carry burdens. Believing that you are alone will hinder your progress; therefore learn to accept help.

CHOOSE JOY AND GRATITUDE

"Be joyful in the Lord," the Bible says, bearing in mind that your joy is from within and reflects whom you believe and concentrate on what you have left rather than the 'spilt milk' you lost. However, if you choose to be bitter, you risk hurting yourself, your children and others

GET PAST YOUR PAST

Turning your single parenthood situation around will only be possible by tenaciously working to make the necessary changes to return to God's original plan for the family.

While others learn from your experience, those caught up in the events need to learn more from their own experience. This applies to both parents and their children. You should become a teacher of your own experience and teach it to whoever is willing to listen. Don't shy away from it or be ashamed. However painful your experience is, it is part of life, or it would never have existed. God's expectation is that we should learn from it so there is no repeat of the unpleasant story. Through the prophet Isaiah, God said,

> *"But forget all that—it is nothing compared to what I am going to do. For I am about to do something new. See, I have already begun! Do you not see it? I will make a pathway through the wilderness. I will create rivers in the dry wasteland."*
>
> — ISAIAH 43:18-19 NLT

Our God, all-knowing as He is, is at the forefront of forgetting the past. He is urging us to forget our past and let Him do a new thing, which in fact He has started. We see this fulfilled in the lives of so many people in the Bible, people who had a very bad past but were forgiven and restored as a result of their turning to God. To mention a few, Rahab (who we referred to earlier) was a harlot and a foreigner in Israel. She heard about the miracles God performed in Egypt and believed and was counted to her as righteousness. She later became one of Jesus' ancestry mothers. Paul, one of the greatest Apostles, went about arresting, jailing, maiming and killing followers of Christ, but when confronted by Jesus on one of his evil missions, surrendered and became the chief Apostle to the Gentiles besides writing almost half of the New Testament by divine revelation. He saw a glimpse of heaven while still alive, according to the Scriptures. It follows, therefore, that when God determines your future, He doesn't consult your past. God, who had used the people mentioned above, flawed as they were, can give you a new beginning. Please bear in mind that it is not possible for you to be in control of your future while still clinging to the past, however good you think it is. So learn from it and let it go.

OVERCOMING LONELINESS AND BUILDING RELATIONSHIPS

Do not allow loneliness to overtake you. Human beings are created to live together. God said, "it is not good that man (Adam) should live alone," and therefore gave him a companion. We, therefore, have two ways of relationship, one with God and the other with human beings. Neither can our jobs, riches nor businesses satisfy us. Loneliness can blind you to your needs. With prayers, set out to make friends and reach out to others in fellowship. Do not be interested in your own life alone but in others too, as those who water other people's fields will be so watered by God. Your responsibility is to find unmet needs and commit yourself to them through which you will overcome your loneliness and start to live again.

An important key to recovery is being thankful at all times. Thank God for your life, health and every blessing you receive every day. Make no mistake; God sees ahead of you and nothing takes Him by surprise. You can make a list of all the good things God has done in your life, so you know how to be grateful and hopeful.

CARING FOR YOURSELF PHYSICALLY, EMOTIONALLY AND FOODWISE

Whether you think about it or not, you are the pillar holding together the whole house. Thanks for the support of the Holy Spirit who is the Chief Bearer of the load. So take good care of yourself if you don't want to experience a collapse of the whole system. Don't overlook any form of weakness, headache, pain or stress. It could be a symptom of a worse situation. Maintain a regular visit to your GP/Doctor and be sure to find time to relax regularly. Exercise is very important. Taking walks is good especially if you drive for most of the time. Most of the exercises we take impact positively on our health as they help to reduce our stress level, while our vital organs like hearts and lungs function very well. Lack of exercise could increase the risk of heart disease, according to medical experts. So if you want to stay fit, keep your body exercised regularly.

It is obvious that we are what we eat. We don't need a magnifier to distinguish a well-balanced eater from one who eats poor-quality food. There are junks all over the place and they are very cheap too. They are just to fill an empty stomach and are of very low quality. To stay healthy your diet must be well-balanced. Your food must be well prepared. Granted that cooking is now hard work, for lack of time and having to work long hours, the benefit of preparing your own food is immeasurable. Cooking your own food assures you of what you are eating. This does not rule out eating out once in a while or buying takeaway. Teach your children very early to eat fruits and vegetables, which most kids find boring, as they grow older. Avoid stocking up on unhealthy snacks. Breakfast is very good as experience shows that kids with food inside their stomachs, as they go to school, concentrate more and perform better than those with empty stomachs. Though some kids don't like to eat breakfast you need to persuade them to eat anyway. Water is very good and children should be encouraged to drink plenty of it especially as they lose much water through running around.

RECOVERY FROM DIVORCE

On Tuesday 16 December 2008, Bob Gass, the Author of *Word for Today* wrote the following about divorce:

> *"Divorce is like amputation: you survive, but it feels like there is less of you. And it's worse if you didn't want the divorce, or feel abandoned by a church that does nothing to help."*

So how can you 'walk through this fire' without being burned? By doing four things.

1. Forgive yourself: *"I ... am he who blots out your transgressions, for my own sake, and remembers your sins no more"* (Isaiah 43:25). God forgives and forgets and He will give you the grace to forgive yourself, too. You also need to love and accept yourself. Remember that you are the only person you cannot get away from, so learn to accept yourself for who you are or you will be miserable. The Bible says to love others as yourself. If you do not love yourself, how can you love others? Only by loving and accepting yourself in God's way will you love others.

2. Forgive those who've hurt you: Forgiveness is the one power you always have over anybody who hurts you. So keep on forgiving, until the past no longer controls you. Make forgiveness your fixed attitude! Only by forgiving and forgetting can you set it down and move on.

3. Take your time: Don't make any big changes right now. You're on an emotional roller coaster, vacillating between wanting them back and wanting them to suffer. You're vulnerable to other people's comments and easily drawn toward anybody who pays you attention. Slow down! Healthy people make healthy choices, so spend time reading God's Word, praying, seeking counsel, and allowing yourself to be made whole.

4. Start giving back: *"... Your God is gracious and compassionate. He will not turn his face from you if you return to him."* (2 Chronicles 30:9). Realising God hasn't turned His back on you, is what enables you to 'Comfort those in any trouble with the comfort you have received from God.' (2 Corinthians 1:4). When the above happens, you're becoming whole, your future is bright and your possibilities unlimited.

CHAPTER 16
OVERCOME YOUR FEAR

What has happened to you may cause you to fear. You feel insecure, inadequate and feel like hiding from people. In order that your fear does not control you, you need to face it squarely. Fear is an evil spirit which you need to resist with the help of the Holy Spirit. When you worry, you anticipate the worst and imagine mountains of potential dangers. This could lead to building walls of defence against non-existing attacks. Learn to replace your fear with promises of God, one of which is,

> *"I can do all things through Christ, who strengthens me."*
>
> — PHILIPPIANS 4:13 NKJV

> *"Be anxious for nothing, but with prayers and thanksgiving bring all your troubles to God, for He cares for you."*
>
> — PHILIPPIANS 4:6 NKJV

Self-criticism calls you to review your past and to judge your own behaviour. You compare yourself to others in a derogatory manner and declare yourself a failure. All of these are potential sources of real failure in the future. If you aim at success, you must learn to replace your critical self-talk with Scriptures. After all, God makes each person in a unique way, and He makes no mistakes. You might have made mistakes, but you are not a mistake, and the best you can do is to start working at being the best God made you. Always remember, when you become a born-again Christian, the Bible says that you are a new person; old things have passed away, including all your past mistakes. You, therefore, need to start your new life as God has designed it.

You must learn to be optimistic. Optimism has been described as a 'true moral courage', which will enable you to motivate your children. You have the task of nurturing their sense of worth. You need to get them involved in everything you do, however young they may be. Be as it may, they are now your closest allies. Engaging them at all times, by seeking their opinion and using it will make them feel a part of the solution to the tasks on hand – which they are in reality. If you fail to enlist their full support, you might be asking for trouble. Just one of them is capable of aggravating your fragile condition, turning it into a nightmare. Therefore seek their cooperation. It is unwise to impose your will on them. This is not to say that your authority should be undermined. No! However, if you keep in mind that the situation you are in now was thrust on them without consulting them (which they know), you will do well not to push them too hard. They are not a bag of potatoes. It is your duty to lighten their burden by showing them understanding, love and kindness, as well as demonstrating your confidence in them. This keeps their hope in God and themselves alive. Assure them that this phase is passing and will not be a permanent feature of their lives The fact is, whether you thought long and hard about the step you took or not, as well as the resultant effect it brings, you, the perpetrator must determine to undo all the consequences, wherever possible, that have been brought upon them. 'It is a task that must be done.'

You may think you are alone; you are not, for God is with you, according to His promise. The promise is yours for taking, provided you choose to see the well by your side rather than craving for the wealth of Father Abraham left behind by Hagar. Nevertheless, this Hagar is no loser in the right sense of it.

When in anger, Sarah, Abraham's wife, demanded that Hagar be cast out with her son, Ishmael, God intervened and gave her a few steps, which every single parent should embrace.

So in Genesis 21:14-21, Abraham and his wife, Sarah, sent Hagar and Ishmael, Abraham and Hagar's son, packing. Hagar wandered aimlessly into the wilderness of Beersheba, and the bottle of water Abraham strapped to her shoulders ran out. She, therefore, left Ishmael in the shade of a bush, walking a few yards away so as not to watch the boy die, and she burst into tears. As could be expected, Ishmael was crying, too, and the Bible says, *"Then God heard the boy's cries."* God, however, had a bigger and better plan for the poor boy. In verse 18, the angel of God called to Hagar from heaven:

> *"Arise, lift up the lad...hold him in thine hand; for I will make him... great."*
>
> — GENESIS 21:18 KJV

Hagar was given four steps that made up the life and destiny of her son. Since both mother and child were down, it was impossible for fallen Hagar to lift her child unless she was on her feet, and so she was encouraged to *"Arise."* As she allowed the Word of God to pull her out of her slum, so also every single parent should be encouraged to rise to the task before him or her.

"Lift up the lad" here is more spiritual than physical. You are to give your children positive reinforcement despite your fallen state. God will equip you to lift up your children if you will let Him. Once your children are lifted up, it will be very difficult for anyone from outside to tear them down. This calls for self-determination to focus on God only and not rely on mere humans whose arms can fail.

The admonition *"hold him in thine hand"* calls for an intimate relationship between you and your children. There should be friendship between you and them and between each other. You should be bonded together in love for one another. The home atmosphere should be free from all tension. Always encourage them and do not hesitate to discipline them when need be, and do not allow criticism to become the order of the day if you don't want to push them out. Be their confidant!

God promised to make Ishmael into a *great* nation, which He fulfilled. As a matter of fact, he sits on a greater percentage of the oil wealth of the world today. God is no respecter of persons. Hagar single-handedly raised her son, and God blessed him tremendously. Just because you are raising your children alone should not be a hindrance to their greatness unless you don't know whom you believe. Your past, with all its mistakes, cannot prevent them from being blessed by God.

Dear single parent, please be the first teacher for your children. If you have to teach them, it follows that you have the knowledge of what you will teach. Knowledge comes by hearing and understanding the concept of a particular subject, and in this case, it should be the Word of God. Teach them from your experiences, so they can avoid all your pitfalls. Rahab, the prostitute and probably a single parent, did not come to Israel to continue with her prostitution. But by putting her faith in the God of Israel, who opened the Red Sea, she settled down and became the wife of Salmon, the great-grandfather of Jesse, the father of King David of Israel. When she abandoned her former trade and embraced the God of Israel, Rahab never knew what her faith would earn her. Single parents, don't let what you have done or what was done to you deny you and your children God's blessings.

The Bible says,

> *"But watch out! Be careful never to forget what you yourself have seen. Do not let these memories escape from your mind as long as you live! And be sure to pass them on to your children and grandchildren."*

— DEUTERONOMY 4:9 NLT

Your children need to hear about the God who saw you through your dark days so that when they encounter difficulties in future, they will put their trust in God. Your testimonies are also your children's testimonies because they are partakers of your suffering, and when God delivered you, they were also delivered. Your wisdom will stay with them for their lifetime.

Your role in their life offers you an opportunity to bring right out of wrong through a heart of forgiveness—forgive yourself and forgive others that might have wronged you. This enables your children to overlook any grudge they have harboured against anyone too. Your heart of forgiveness will pave the way for God's blessing for you and your children. Whatever has been done to you is not an excuse for you to carry unresolved issues of the past into your future. Your yesteryears are now irrelevant to your tomorrow. Start a brand new life in obedience to the Word of God, which admonishes us to forget the former things so that new things can emerge (Isaiah 43:18-19). Don't miss your beautiful tomorrow by clinging to your ugly past of guilt, bitterness, pain, hopelessness and unforgiveness.

CHAPTER 17
WISDOM: THE ESSENTIAL REQUIREMENT FOR EVERY SINGLE PARENT

WHAT IS WISDOM?

Apostle James offers us some insight. He writes,

> *"Who is wise and understanding among you? Let him show by good conduct that his works are done in the meekness of wisdom. But if you have bitter envy and self-seeking in your hearts, do not boast and lie against the truth. This wisdom does not descend from above, but is earthly, sensual, demonic. For where envy and self-seeking exist, confusion and every evil thing are there. But the wisdom that is from above is first pure, then peaceable, gentle, willing to yield, full*

of mercy and good fruits, without partiality and without hypocrisy."

— JAMES 3:13-17 NKJV

The greatest need of single parents is the wisdom that comes from the Father of Light. As quoted above, there are other kinds of worldly wisdom given by the ruler of darkness, however, such wisdom will only lead people into destruction.

UNLOCKING THE WISDOM FROM THE WORD OF GOD

Every individual, including single parents, requires deliverance through the Word. Every essential necessity lies within the Word. The Bible identifies the Word of God as God Himself (John 1:1). Hence, the Word of God encompasses attributes such as the Spirit, power, light, fire, sword, hammer, life, and much more. In the Word, we possess all-encompassing resources.

We gain access to these attributes by diligent study of the Word and the judicious application of its virtues. Undoubtedly, our faith plays a pivotal role in determining our blessings from God. This becomes particularly crucial for single parents aiming to effectively raise their children.

Without these *powers*, alternative forms of assistance would prove inadequate.

These endowed attributes empower you to receive aid from unexpected sources, including people and nations previously unknown to you. Possessing the Word equips you comprehensively for progression in every aspect of life.

EMBRACING ACCEPTANCE

Just as God loves other types of sinners and wants them to come to repentance, single parents are no exception. We have all fallen short of His grace and mercy. Single parents, therefore, need acceptance, not for what has befallen them but for being part of God's creation, which He says He doesn't want destroyed. Christ, who knows no sin could accept every sinner that comes to Him, others who are battling with one sin or the other, ought to accommodate those whose sin is different from theirs, as the Bible says that 'we are all sinners forgiven by Christ through His cross'.

PURSUING HEALING

Single parents and their children, who have endured violence within the same household as couples and families, followed by a succession of separations, as well as the strains and pressures of divorce proceedings, accompanied by various forms of public embarrassment in the community, workplaces, schools, shopping centres, and social gatherings, have undoubtedly experienced tremendous challenges. Their circumstances, by the grace of God, evoke only empathy and patience, nothing less.

EXTENDING PATIENCE AND UNDERSTANDING

How frequently do we find ourselves growing impatient with those whose behaviour doesn't align with our own? Ironically, we often pass judgment on individuals, assuming we possess all the pertinent facts—an impossible feat. Similar to how Job's friends misjudged him in the face of his trials instead of offering empathy, we too can fall into the trap of unjust accusations and hasty judgments.

Colossians 3:12 encourages the adoption of qualities like tender mercies, kindness, humility, meekness, and longsuffering—qualities that may have been lacking in these individuals' previous circumstances. As fellow believers, we are called to extend patience and understanding to them, recognising that we are not always privy to the burdens others may be carrying.

CHAPTER 18
RECONCILIATION

Reconciliation is the true evidence of forgiveness. First, the reconciliation with Christ that everyone involved in estranged or broken relationships must experience. Apostle Paul writes,

> *"All this is from God, who reconciled us to himself through Christ and gave us the ministry of reconciliation: that God was reconciling the world to himself in Christ, not counting people's sins against them. And he has committed to us the message of reconciliation. We are therefore Christ's ambassadors, as though God were making his appeal through us. We implore you on Christ's behalf: Be reconciled to God."*
>
> — 2 CORINTHIANS 5:18-20 NIV

God reconciled us first to Himself in Christ and then commissions us to reconcile others to him. We cannot fulfil this ministry if we harbour bitterness and hatred towards anyone. So to be free from the bitter past, we should seek reconciliation prayerfully.

The children are likely to play a big role, but we also have to sow the seed in them so that everyone can heal and reconcile through the love of Christ. This may not necessarily mean restoration back to how things were originally —which may be impossible in many cases—nevertheless, it is vital and requires grace. However, it has to be intentional. This is most important as we look forward to our everlasting home. The writer of Hebrews says,

> *"Follow peace with all men, and holiness, without which no man shall see the Lord: Looking diligently lest any man fail of the grace of God; lest any root of bitterness springing up trouble you, and thereby many be defiled."*
>
> — HEBREWS 12:14-15 KJV

For fresh breakups, reconciliation must never be ruled out and with the support of every well-meaning relation, this should be pursued—especially with the foreknowledge of impending challenges enumerated in this book. Whatever is possible to avoid break-ups or to ensure that reconciliation is pursued before it becomes too late should be applied. This brings us back to the original opening statements of this book:

> God designed the family to be comprised of a father and mother—male and female—and we must work to keep it so.

May we enjoy His help as we pursue this in Jesus' Name. Amen.

ABOUT THE BOOK

This empowering book, *Single Parenting: Wisdom and Hope for the Journey,* delves deep into the challenges, triumphs, and transformative experiences that single parents face as they navigate the often tumultuous waters of raising children alone. The book takes readers on a comprehensive exploration of the various aspects of single parenthood. From understanding the emotional rollercoaster of loss and grief to finding strength in faith and wisdom, the book offers practical guidance and a wealth of spiritual insight for those treading this unique path. *Single Parenting: Wisdom and Hope for the Journey* is a powerful resource that combines spiritual wisdom, practical guidance, and heartfelt encouragement for those journeying through the complexities of single parenthood. It offers a guiding light for both single parents and individuals seeking to engage with wisdom and empathy when interacting with the single parents within their sphere of influence.

ABOUT THE AUTHOR

Augusta Adesola Ogunyemi is a mother, grandmother, and great-grandmother. She became a single mother at the age of 35, with five children aged between 2 years and 11 years. In this book, she draws upon her experience as a single parent, her deep faith in God, and her professional knowledge of Sociology.

Printed in Great Britain
by Amazon